fondues

fondues

over 160 step-by-step recipes

BARNES & NOBLE BOOKS

NEW YORK

This edition published by Barnes & Noble, Inc.,
by arrangement with Salamander Books Ltd.

2002, 2003, 2004 Barnes and Noble Books

ISBN 0-7607-3360-0

M 10 9 8 7 6 5 4 3

© Salamander Books Ltd., 2002

An imprint of **Chrysalis** Books Group plc

A CIP catalog record for this book is available from the
Library of Congress.

All correspondence concerning the contents of this book should
be addressed to Salamander Books Ltd.

CREDITS
Project managed by Stella Caldwell
Editor: Madeline Weston
Filmset by SX Composing DTP, England
Printed in China

CONTENTS

INTRODUCTION

The word fondue comes from the French word *fondre*, to melt. It was in the French speaking area of Switzerland that the cheese fondue originated many centuries ago. During the harsh Alpine winters Swiss peasants had very limited food apart from cheese and bread, and they had few cooking utensils, so melting the cheese in one pot was a good way of using up the rather dry odds and ends of cheese. The cheese fondue became widely known outside Switzerland when people began to take ski-ing holidays and enjoyed a fondue or raclette after a hard day on the slopes.

Many countries around the world have developed their own version of the fondue. The classic fondue Bourguignonne, where strips of steak are cooked in hot oil, is very popular in France, while in the Far East pieces of meat, fish or chicken are cooked in boiling stock along with vegetables. Afterwards, noodles are added to the stock which is then served up as a soup.

The fondue, extremely popular in the 1970s, is making a welcome return to the stylish dinner table, and today there are a large number of different types of fondue sets available on the market. A fondue set will usually consist of a pot, a stand on which the pot rests, and a burner for cooking or keeping the food hot. In addition to this, they often come with a set of four or six long-handled forks. The burner either contains a pad which needs to be impregnated with methylated spirits, or a foil container of gel is placed in the burner. They will usually have a sliding cover over the burner - this enables you to adjust the size of the flame and thereby regualte the tempertaure. A cover is also usually provided for snuffing out the flame when cooking has been completed. Small chocolate fondue pots make use of a candle to provide a gentle heat. It is extremely important

that the base containing the burner is very stable and it needs to be placed on a thick mat on the table.

The traditional cheese fondue pot resembles the original Swiss *caquelon*; it is wide and quite shallow and usually made of earthenware and sometimes light metal such as copper. These pots are not suitable for a meat fondue as they are too open and shallow for hot oil or stock. It is quite easy to overheat the metal pots, which will cause the cheese to catch and burn.

A traditional meat fondue pot is taller and narrower, but most fondue

Left: Large stainless steel fondue pot

pots sold nowadays tend to be this shape and they are suitable for either meat or cheese fondues. Cast iron pots are typically the most expensive on the market, but they are the best quality as it is much easier to keep a steady temperature with cast iron. Another advantage is that the weight of the cast iron sets makes them more stable.

Chocolate fondue sets are smaller in size but it is not necessary to have a special pot as an attractive bowl over a nightlight works just as well. A chocolate fondue set can be very useful for keeping sauces warm at the table. Similar to a chocolate fondue set is a special pot for making Bagna Cauda, and again, this is heated with the aid of a nightlight. These pots are most frequently made of terracotta.

A Mongolian hotpot or steamboat is a traditional pot in which Oriental fondues are made. They are manufactured of brass or aluminum, and consist of a rounded pot which has a funnel running down the center of it. This is set over a burner into which hot charcoal is placed. Boiling stock is used and the burner ensures it is kept bubbling throughout the meal.

Long handled forks are essential pieces of equipment for spearing whatever food is being dipped into the fondue. They most often have colored handles or a colored mark on the end so that each diner can readily identify their own fork. The food is transferred to a dinner plate, and dipped

Above: Small chocolate fondue pot

into one of the sauces with an eating fork before eating. This is not just for hygiene reasons, but also to prevent people burning themselves - of particular importance when dipping food into hot oil. As an alternative to forks, bamboo skewers can also be used. Little Chinese wire baskets are used with Mongolian hotpots but they also come in useful for dipping food such as meatballs, fishcakes or anything else which might be too fragile to stay on a fork.

Six is the maximum number of people which can safely and comfortably share one fondue pot, so for parties of eight or more it would be necessary to have two pots on the go simultaneously. For increased speed, make the cheese fondue on top of the stove before transferring it to the burner. Also heat oil or stock on top of the stove and for obvious reasons take great care when transferring the fondue pot to the burner.

CHEESE FONDUES

Choose a strongly flavored cheese and always allow it to melt slowly. You need to have alcohol in a cheese fondue. Not only does it improve the flavor, but it lowers the boiling point and stops the protein in the cheese from curdling. Do not worry if the mixture looks lumpy and separates; keep stirring and it will gradually become smooth, but do not be tempted to turn the heat up as this will probably overcook and spoil the fondue. If the mixture becomes too thick, add a little warmed wine or cider. Encourage diners to stir the fondue right down to the bottom when they dip their bread in; this helps to keep it smooth and creamy. When the fondue is nearly finished there will

Right:
Cast iron
fondue pot
with spirit burner

usually be a crisp crust on the bottom off the pot. Scrape it out and divide it between the guests - it tastes wonderful and is regarded as a treat. Make use of day-old bread for dipping as it will not be too crumbly, and always cut the bread so that each portion has some crust on to make spearing with a fork easier. If anybody does drop their bread in the fondue, tradition dictates that they have to perform a forfeit. Ladies have to kiss the man next to them and a man is obliged to buy the next round of drinks!

MEAT, FISH AND SEAFOOD FONDUES

It is important to have all the ingredients and accompaniments that you will need prepared in advance; this makes your task much easier. The meat should be cut and arranged attractively on plates, sauces need to be prepared and placed in small pots, and salads should be ready for dressing just before cooking commences. If using oil, vegetable oil is recommended, but a little flavored oil can be added if you like. For safety reasons, the fondue pot should not be filled more than half full as the hot oil can easily bubble up when the meat is dipped in. Heat the oil to 350-375F, but if you do not have a thermometer to hand, there is an quick and easy test which you can perform with the help of a piece of day-old bread. Dip a small cube into the oil; it will turn golden in about 30 seconds if the oil is at the correct temperature. Be careful not to add too much food to the oil at once. This will have the adverse effect of lowering the temperature of the oil and the food will consequently not cook properly. Be sure to dry meat and fish thoroughly on kitchen paper before cooking in hot oil, otherwise the oil will spit.

DESSERT FONDUES

Most dessert fondues tend to be made of chocolate, but creamy fruit purées are popular too. Melted chocolate is luxurious, silky-smooth and offers a great feel-good factor. It always pays to choose the best quality - for cooking purposes, a rich, dark chocolate is recommended. Always check the label for cocoa-solid content, and never go below 50 per cent. Take great care when melting the chocolate, especially if it is white chocolate, as it will solidify into clumps if overheated. Melting the chocolate with cream solves this problem and makes for a delicious mixture!

If you are dipping cake into the fondue, freshly baked cake can be a little too crumbly. Day-old cake works best, so if you are planning to make one of the dessert fondues with small cakes or cake slices, it is a good idea to prepare them the day before. If you are dipping fruit, choose firm pieces and, if possible, chill them first as the chocolate will coat them more effectively when they are cold.

CHEESE

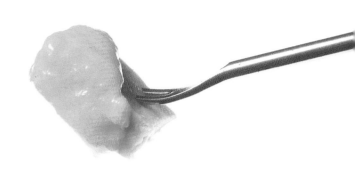

FONDUE SAVOYARDE

1 clove garlic, halved
⅔ cup dry white wine
1 teaspoon lemon juice
2 cups grated Gruyère cheese
2 cups grated Emmental cheese
1 tablespoon cornstarch
2 tablespoons kirsch
pinch freshly grated nutmeg
pinch cayenne pepper
TO SERVE:
cubes of baguette
green salad
slices of air dried ham

Rub cut side of garlic round inside fondue pot.

Pour wine and lemon juice into the pot and place over a low heat. Heat gently until bubbling. Gradually stir in grated cheeses and heat gently, stirring, until completely melted. In a small bowl, blend together the cornstarch and kirsch, and stir into cheese mixture.

Continue to cook, stirring, for 2-3 minutes until mixture is thick and creamy. Add nutmeg and cayenne pepper. Transfer pot to the lighted spirit burner. To serve, spear cubes of bread on to the fondue forks and dip into cheese mixture. Serve with the salad and air dried ham.

Serves 4-6.

DEVILED CHEESE FONDUE

1 clove garlic, cut in half
¼ cup milk
3 cups grated Applewood smoked Cheddar cheese
6 teaspoons all-purpose flour
1 teaspoon prepared mustard
2 teaspoons Worcestershire sauce
2 teaspoons horseradish relish
cubes of ham and toasted granary bread, to serve

Rub the inside of the fondue pot with the cut clove of garlic, then add milk and heat until bubbling.

Toss the cheese in the flour, then add to the pot and stir all the time over a low heat until it is melted and mixture is thick and smooth.

Stir in the mustard, Worcestershire sauce, and horseradish relish. Serve with cubes of ham and cubes of toasted granary bread.

Serves 4-6.

CLASSIC SWISS FONDUE

1 clove garlic, halved
1 cup dry white wine
1 teaspoon lemon juice
2 cups grated Gruyère cheese
2 cups grated Emmental cheese
2 teaspoons cornstarch
2 tablespoons kirsch
pinch white pepper
pinch freshly grated nutmeg
cubes of French bread, to serve

Rub the inside of the fondue pot with cut clove of garlic.

Pour in wine and lemon juice and heat gently until boiling. Reduce the heat to low and gradually stir in grated cheese with a wooden spoon, then continue to heat until cheeses melt, stirring frequently.

In a small bowl, blend cornstarch smoothly with kirsch, then stir in cheese mixture and continue to cook for 2-3 minutes until mixture of thick and smooth, stirring frequently. Do not allow fondue to boil. Season with pepper and nutmeg. Serve with cubes of French bread.

Serves 4-6.

GOUDA CHEESE FONDUE

½ small onion
2 teaspoons cumin seeds
⅔ cup dry white wine
1 teaspoon lemon juice
3½ cups grated Gouda cheese
2 teaspoons cornstarch
2 tablespoons gin
freshly ground black pepper
pinch nutmeg
light rye bread cubes, to serve

Rub inside of the fondue pot with cut side of onion. Place cumin seeds in pot and heat gently for 1 minute.
Add wine and lemon juice. Heat until nearly

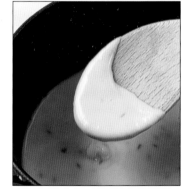

boiling and then add grated cheese. Heat gently, stirring, until cheese melts. In a small bowl blend together cornstarch and gin. Stir into cheese mixture.

As soon as fondue thickens and comes just to a simmer, take off the heat. Season with pepper and nutmeg. Place the fondue pot over the lighted spirit burner and serve with the rye bread.

Serves 4.

FONDUE INDIENNE

1 clove garlic, halved
3 cups grated Cheddar cheese
2 tablespoons all-purpose flour
1 small onion, grated
1½ cups dry white wine
2 teaspoons curry paste
2 tablespoons mango chutney
salt and freshly ground black pepper
cayenne pepper, to garnish
naan bread, to serve

Rub the inside of the fondue pot with the cut clove of garlic. Crush the garlic.

Place cheese and flour in a plastic bag and toss to combine. Place crushed garlic, onion, wine, and curry paste in the fondue pot and bring almost to a simmer. Gradually stir in cheese, allowing it to melt between each addition.

Stir in mango chutney, and salt and pepper to taste. Place on the lighted spirit burner. Sprinkle a little cayenne pepper over. Serve with pieces of naan bread.

Serves 4.

Note: If the mango chutney has large pieces of fruit in it, chop it finely.

SMOKY GERMAN FONDUE

½ small onion
1 cup light ale
3 cups grated German smoked cheese
1 cup grated Emmental cheese
3 teaspoons cornstarch
3 tablespoons milk
1 teaspoon German mustard
rye bread and cooked frankfurters, to serve

Rub the inside of the fondue pot with cut side of onion.

Pour in light ale and heat gently until boiling. Reduce the heat to low and gradually stir in the grated cheeses, then continue to heat until cheeses melt, stirring frequently.

In a small bowl, blend cornstarch smoothly with milk, stir into cheese with mustard, and continue to cook for 2-3 minutes until mixture is thick and creamy, stirring frequently. Serve with cubes of rye bread and pieces of cooked frankfurters.

Serves 4-6.

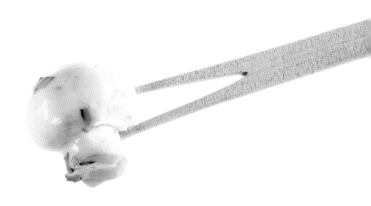

SOMERSET FONDUE

½ small onion
1 cup dry cider
1 teaspoon lemon juice
3 cups grated Cheddar cheese
½ teaspoon dry mustard
3 teaspoons cornstarch
3 tablespoons apple juice
pinch white pepper
wedges of apple and cubes of crusty bread, to serve

Rub the inside of the fondue pot with cut side of onion.

Pour in cider and lemon juice and heat gently until boiling. Reduce the heat to low and gradually stir in grated cheese, then continue to heat until cheese melts, stirring frequently.

In a small bowl, blend mustard and cornstarch smoothly with apple juice. Stir into cheese mixture and continue to cook for 2-3 minutes until mixture is thick and creamy, stirring frequently. Season with pepper. Serve with wedges of apple and cubes of crusty bread.

Serves 4-6.

FRENCH BRIE FONDUE

13oz ripe French Brie
¼ cup butter
1 onion, finely chopped
1 clove garlic, crushed
¼ cup all-purpose flour
1¼ cups chicken or vegetable stock
⅔ cup heavy cream
1 tablespoon chopped fresh tarragon
salt and freshly ground black pepper
TO SERVE:
grapes
cubes of French bread
raw button mushrooms

Cut away rind from Brie and slice cheese thinly. Set aside.

Melt butter in the fondue pot over a low heat. Add onion and garlic, and cook gently for 10 minutes until softened. Sprinkle flour over and cook for 1-2 minutes, stirring. Gradually add stock and continue to stir until mixture thickens. Simmer gently for 2-3 minutes.

Stir sliced Brie and cream into the fondue. Cook, stirring, until cheese has melted and mixture is smooth. Stir in tarragon and season with salt and pepper. Transfer the fondue pot to the lighted spirit burner. To serve, spear grapes, bread, and mushrooms on to skewers or fondue forks and dip into the fondue.

Serves 4-6.

SMOKY CHEESE & HAM FONDUE

1 cup grated Gruyère cheese
2 cups grated smoked Cheddar cheese
1 tablespoon cornstarch
1 tablespoon butter
1 small onion, finely chopped
1 clove garlic, crushed
⅔ cup dry white wine
½ teaspoon smoked paprika
4oz smoked ham, chopped
TO SERVE:
wedges of apple
cubes of crusty bread

In a bowl, toss together the grated cheese and the cornstarch.

In a saucepan, melt butter over a low heat. Add onion and garlic and cook gently for 10 minutes until softened. Place wine in the fondue pot and heat gently until boiling. Gradually stir in grated cheeses and heat gently, stirring, until completely melted.

Stir in onion and garlic, then paprika and ham, and cook for a few more minutes until thick and smooth. Transfer the fondue pot to the lighted spirit burner. To serve, spear apple and bread on to skewers or fondue forks and dip into the fondue.

Serves 4.

CHEESE & ONION FONDUE

6 teaspoons butter
1 large onion, very finely chopped
2 teaspoons all-purpose flour
⅔ cup thick sour cream
2 cups grated Gruyère cheese
2 cups grated Cheddar cheese
2 tablespoons chopped fresh chives
freshly ground black pepper
small cooked potatoes and small cooked sausages, to serve

Melt butter in a saucepan, add onion and cook for 4-5 minutes until soft but not brown.

Stir in flour, then add thick sour cream and cook for 2 minutes. Continue to cook whilst adding cheeses and heat until mixture is smooth, stirring frequently.

Add chives and season with pepper. Pour into the fondue pot and serve with small cooked potatoes and small cooked sausages.

Serves 4-6.

BLUE CHEESE FONDUE

1 cup milk
1 cup cream cheese
2 cups grated Danish Blue cheese
½ teaspoon garlic salt
3 teaspoons cornstarch
2 tablespoons light cream
cubes of ham or garlic sausage and cubes of crusty
  bread, to serve

Put milk and cream cheese into the fondue pot and, with an electric mixer, beat until creamy and smooth.

Place fondue pot over a gentle heat and gradually stir in the blue cheese, then continue to heat until smooth, stirring.

Blend garlic salt and cornstarch smoothly with cream; stir into cheese and cook for a further 2-3 minutes until thick and creamy, stirring frequently. Serve with cubes of ham or garlic sausage, and cubes of crusty bread.

Serves 4-6.

CIDER FONDUE

½ small onion
1¼ cups dry cider
1 teaspoon lemon juice
4 cups grated farmhouse Cheddar cheese
1 tablespoon cornstarch
2 tablespoons dry sherry
pinch mustard powder
1 teaspoon Worcestershire sauce
1 teaspoon chopped fresh sage
salt and freshly ground black pepper
TO SERVE:
cubes of crusty farmhouse bread
wedges of apple
celery sticks
pickle

Rub inside of the fondue pot with cut side of onion. Place cider and lemon juice in fondue pot and heat gently until boiling. Gradually stir in grated cheese and heat gently, stirring, until completely melted. In a small bowl, blend together cornstarch and sherry. Add mustard and Worcestershire sauce. Stir into cheese mixture.

Continue to cook, stirring until thick and smooth. Stir in sage, and season with salt and pepper. Transfer the fondue pot to the lighted spirit burner. To serve, spear bread on to fondue forks to dip into fondue and serve accompanied by apple, celery, and pickle.

Serves 6.

ITALIAN PESTO FONDUE

DUTCH FONDUE

1 clove garlic
scant 1 cup Soave wine
2 cups grated Gruyère cheese
1½ cups dolcelatte cheese, cubed
½ cup grated Parmesan cheese
1 tablespoon cornstarch
2 tablespoons milk
1 tablespoon pesto sauce
salt and freshly ground black pepper
TO SERVE:
foccacia and ciabatta bread cut into cubes
slices of salami
olives

½ small onion
1 cup milk
4 cups grated Gouda cheese
2 teaspoons caraway seeds
3 teaspoons cornstarch
3 tablespoons gin
freshly ground black pepper
light rye bread and button mushrooms, to serve

Rub the inside of the fondue pot with cut side of onion.

Cut clove of garlic in half and rub cut side round the inside of the fondue pot. (See above.) Place wine in the fondue pot and heat gently until boiling. Gradually stir in prepared cheeses and heat gently, stirring, until completely melted. In a small bowl, blend together the cornstarch and milk. Stir into the cheese mixture. Continue to cook, stirring, until thick and smooth.

Add milk and heat until boiling, then gradually stir in cheese. Continue to heat until cheese melts, stirring frequently.

Stir in pesto, and season with salt and pepper. Transfer the fondue pot to the lighted spirit burner. To serve, spear bread and salami on to fondue forks to dip into the fondue, and serve accompanied by the olives.

Serves 6.

VARIATION: Instead of bread and salami, serve cooked tortelloni to dip into the fondue.

Stir in caraway seeds. In a small bowl, blend cornstarch smoothly with gin, then stir into cheese mixture and cook for 2-3 minutes until smooth and creamy, stirring frequently. Season with pepper. Serve with cubes of rye bread and mushrooms.

Serves 4-6.

FONDUE ITALIENNE

1 clove garlic
1¼ cups milk
2 cups grated Mozzarella cheese
2 cups dolcelatte cheese, chopped
½ cup finely grated Parmesan cheese
2 teaspoons cornstarch
3 tablespoons dry white wine
salami, breadsticks, and olives, to serve

Rub the inside of the fondue pot with cut clove of garlic. Add milk and heat until bubbling.

Stir in all the cheeses and continue to heat until melted, stirring frequently.

Blend cornstarch smoothly with wine, stir into cheese mixture and cook for 2-3 minutes until thick and creamy, stirring frequently. Serve with slices of rolled up salami or cubes of salami, breadsticks, and olives.

Serves 4-6.

SPANISH FONDUE

1 clove garlic
generous 1 cup dry Spanish white wine
2 cups grated Gruyère cheese
2 cups grated Manchego cheese
1 tablespoon cornstarch
2 tablespoons dry sherry
2 teaspoons smoked Spanish paprika
salt and freshly ground black pepper
TO SERVE:
chunks of chorizo sausage
pieces of red bell pepper
cubes of crusty country bread
olives
cubes of membrillo (quince paste)

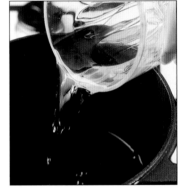

Cut clove of garlic in half and rub the cut side round inside of the fondue pot. Place wine in the fondue pot and heat gently until bubbling. (See above.) Gradually stir in the prepared cheeses and heat gently, stirring, until completely melted. In a small bowl, blend together cornstarch and sherry. Stir into the cheese mixture. Continue to cook, stirring until thick and smooth.

Stir in paprika and season with salt and pepper. Transfer the fondue pot to the lighted spirit burner. To serve, spear chorizo sausage, bell pepper, and bread on to fondue forks to dip into the fondue; serve accompanied by olives and membrillo.

Serves 4-6.

HIGHLAND FONDUE

1 small onion, finely chopped
3 teaspoons butter
1 cup milk
4 cups grated Scottish or mature Cheddar cheese
3 teaspoons cornstarch
4 tablespoons Scotch whisky
cubes of rye and onion bread, to serve

Put onion and butter into a saucepan and cook over a gentle heat until soft. Add milk and heat until boiling.

Gradually stir in cheese and continue to cook until melted, stirring frequently.

In a small bowl, blend cornstarch smoothly with whisky, then stir into cheese mixture and cook 2-3 minutes until thickened, stirring frequently. Pour into the fondue pot and serve with cubes of rye and onion bread.

Serves 4-6.

WELSH RAREBIT FONDUE

1 tablespoon butter
1 small onion, finely chopped
1½ cups light ale
2 cups grated Caerphilly cheese
1 cup grated Welsh Cheddar cheese
1 tablespoon cornstarch
2 tablespoons milk
1 teaspoon Dijon mustard
1 teaspoon Worcestershire sauce
pinch cayenne pepper
salt and freshly ground black pepper
thick slices of toast, cut into cubes, to serve

Place butter in the fondue pot and melt over a low heat.

Add onion, and cook gently for 10 minutes until softened. Add light ale, and heat gently until bubbling. Gradually stir in grated cheeses, and heat gently, stirring, until completely melted. In a small bowl, mix together the cornstarch and milk. Stir into cheese mixture.

Continue to cook, stirring, until thick and smooth. Stir in mustard, Worcestershire sauce, and cayenne pepper. Season with salt and pepper. Transfer the fondue pot to the lighted spirit burner. To serve, spear cubes of toasted bread on fondue forks and dip into fondue.

Serves 4-6.

ISRAELI FONDUE

2 avocados, halved and stones removed
3 teaspoons lemon juice
1 clove garlic, halved
¾ cup dry white wine
3 cups grated Edam cheese
2 teaspoons cornstarch
5 tablespoons smetana or thick sour cream
cubes of sesame-coated French bread and red and
   green bell pepper, to serve

Scoop out flesh from avocados into a bowl and mash until smooth with lemon juice.

Rub the inside of fondue pot with cut side of garlic, then pour in wine and heat until boiling. Over a gentle heat, stir in cheese and cook until melted, stirring frequently.

In a small bowl, blend cornstarch smoothly with smetana or sour cream, then add to cheese mixture with mashed avocados. Continue to cook for 4-5 minutes until thick and smooth, stirring frequently. Serve with cubes of bread and red and green bell pepper.

Serves 4-6.

WELSH FONDUE

6 teaspoons butter
8oz leeks, finely chopped
6 teaspoons all-purpose flour
1 cup lager
2½ cups grated Caerphilly cheese
freshly ground black pepper
cubes of crusty bread, to serve

Put butter into a saucepan and melt over a low heat. Add leeks, cover pan, and cook gently for 10 minutes until tender.

Stir in flour and cook for 1 minute, then add lager and heat until thickened, stirring all the time.

Gradually add cheese and continue to cook until melted, stirring frequently. Season with pepper. Pour into a fondue pot and serve with cubes of crusty bread.

Serves 4-6.

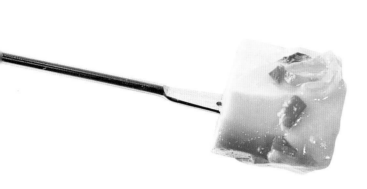

MEXICAN CHILI FONDUE

4 cups grated Monterey Jack cheese
2 tablespoons cornstarch
1 clove garlic
generous 1 cup Mexican lager
1 tablespoon lime juice
1-2 fresh red chilies, seeded and finely chopped
salt and freshly ground black pepper
1 tablespoon chopped fresh cilantro
FRIED SHALLOTS:
8 shallots, thinly sliced
4 tablespoons vegetable oil
TO SERVE:
pickled jalapeño chilies
tomato wedges
cubes of avocado
warm flour tortillas

DANISH FONDUE

6oz bacon, rind removed and finely chopped
1 small onion, finely chopped
3 teaspoons butter
3 teaspoons all-purpose flour
1 cup lager
2 cups grated Havarti cheese
2 cups grated Samso cheese
small sweet and sour gherkins and chunks of light
  rye bread, to serve

Put bacon, onion, and butter into a saucepan
and cook until bacon is golden and onion is
soft.

Make the fried shallots. Heat oil in a skillet,
add shallots, and cook, stirring, for 5 minutes
or until browned. (See above.) Drain on
kitchen paper and set aside. In a bowl, toss
together the grated cheese and the
cornstarch. Cut clove of garlic in half and
rub cut side round inside of the fondue pot.
Add lager, lime juice, and chilies, and heat
gently until boiling.

Stir in flour, then gradually add lager and
cook until thickened, stirring frequently.

Gradually stir in grated cheese and cook
gently, stirring, until completely melted.
Season with salt and pepper. Stir in chopped
cilantro and fried shallots. Transfer the
fondue pot to the lighted spirit burner. Cut
tortillas into strips, roll up, and spear on to
fondue forks to dip into the fondue, with the
jalapeño chilies, tomato, and avocado.

Serves 4-6.

Add cheeses, stirring all the time, and
continue cooking until cheeses have melted
and mixture is smooth. Pour into a fondue
pot and serve with gherkins and chunks of
light rye bread.

Serves 4-6.

CREAMY HERB & GARLIC FONDUE

1 clove garlic
⅔ cup dry white wine
1 tablespoon cornstarch
1¼ cups crème fraîche
1¼ cups full-fat soft cheese with garlic and herbs
pinch freshly grated nutmeg
salt and freshly ground black pepper
1 tablespoon chopped fresh chives
TO SERVE:
cubes of French bread
cherry tomatoes
button mushrooms

Cut clove of garlic in half and rub the cut side round the inside of the fondue pot.

Pour ½ cup of the wine into the fondue pot and heat gently until boiling. In a small bowl, blend cornstarch with the remaining wine. Add to the fondue pot and cook, stirring, until thickened. Reduce the heat and add crème fraîche and soft cheese. Stir until cheese has melted.

Add nutmeg and season with salt and pepper. Sprinkle with chopped chives, and transfer the fondue pot to the lighted spirit burner. To serve, spear bread, tomatoes, and mushrooms on to fondue forks and dip into the fondue.

Serves 4-6.

FONDUE NORMANDE

1 clove garlic, halved
½ cup dry white wine
⅔ cup light cream
12oz Camembert cheese, rind removed
3 teaspoons cornstarch
4 tablespoons Calvados brandy
cubes of French bread and chunks of apple, to serve

Rub the inside of fondue pot with cut side of garlic. Pour in wine and cream and heat until boiling.

Cut cheese into small pieces, then add to the pot and stir over a gentle heat until melted.

In a small bowl, blend cornstarch smoothly with Calvados, then add to cheese mixture and continue to cook for 2-3 minutes until thick and creamy, stirring frequently. Serve with cubes of French bread and chunks of apple.

Serves 4-6.

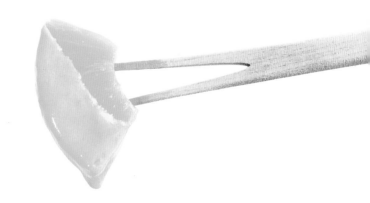

CELEBRATION FONDUE

CHILDREN'S PARTY FONDUE

1 clove garlic, halved
1 cup sparkling white wine
1 cup grated Emmental cheese
3 cups grated Saint Paulin cheese
2 egg yolks
4 tablespoons light cream
2 teaspoons cornstarch
2 tablespoons brandy
Bresaola and cubes of French bread, to serve

Rub the inside of fondue pot with cut clove of garlic. Add wine and heat until boiling.

Gradually add cheeses and heat until melting, then beat in egg yolks and cream.

In a small bowl, blend cornstarch smoothly with brandy, then add to cheese mixture and continue to cook, stirring all the time, until the fondue is thick and creamy. Serve with rolls of Bresaola and cubes of bread.

Serves 4-6.

2 tablespoons butter
¼ cup all-purpose flour
2 cups milk
½ cup cream cheese
1½ cups grated Edam cheese
½ cup heavy cream
½ teaspoon dry mustard
salt and freshly ground black pepper
TO SERVE:
carrot and celery sticks
cherry tomatoes
scallions
wedges of apple
pineapple cubes
cooked baby potatoes

Arrange vegetables and fruit on individual serving plates. Place butter in the fondue pot and heat until melted. (See above.) Stir in flour and cook, stirring, for 1 minute. Gradually stir in milk, then bring to a boil and cook, stirring, until thickened and smooth. Stir in cream cheese, Edam cheese, and cream. Heat gently, stirring, until cheese has melted and mixture is smooth.

Stir in mustard, and season with salt and pepper. Transfer the fondue pot to the lighted spirit burner. To serve, spear vegetables and fruit on to fondue forks and dip into the fondue.

Serves 5-6.

CRICKETER'S FONDUE

3 teaspoons butter
1 small onion, finely chopped
1 cup light ale
4 cups grated Leicestershire cheese
4 teaspoons cornstarch
5 tablespoons light cream
cauliflower flowerets, radishes, and mushrooms, to
serve

Heat butter in a saucepan, add onion, and cook gently until soft. Pour in ale and heat until boiling.

Over a low heat, stir in the cheese and continue to heat until cheese has melted, stirring frequently.

In a small bowl, blend cornstarch smoothly with cream, add to cheese mixture, and cook for 2-3 minutes until smooth and thickened, stirring frequently. Pour into a fondue pot. Serve with cauliflower flowerets, radishes, and mushrooms.

Serves 4-6.

ROSÉ FONDUE

1 clove garlic, halved
1 cup rosé wine
1 cup grated Gruyère cheese
2 cups grated red-veined Cheddar cheese
3 teaspoons cornstarch
2 tablespoons kirsch
cubes of sesame-coated French bread, to serve

Rub the inside of the fondue pot with cut side of garlic. Add wine and heat until boiling.

Gradually stir in cheeses and continue to heat gently until melted, stirring frequently.

In a small bowl, blend cornstarch smoothly with kirsch and stir into cheese mixture. Cook for 2-3 minutes until smooth and thickened, stirring frequently. Serve with cubes of French bread.

Serves 4-6.

PLOUGHMAN'S FONDUE

1 clove garlic, halved
1¼ cups beer
2 cups grated Red Leicester cheese or orange-colored
   Cheddar
2 cups grated Cheddar cheese
3 teaspoons all-purpose flour
1 teaspoon dry mustard
freshly ground black pepper
cubes of granary of white bread and pickles, to serve

Rub the inside of the fondue pot with cut clove of garlic. Add beer and heat until boiling.

Toss grated cheeses in the flour and mustard until well combined.

Over a low heat, add cheeses to the beer and continue to heat, stirring all the time until mixture is smooth. Season with pepper. Serve with cubes of granary or white bread and pickles.

Serves 4-6.

CRUNCHY CAMEMBERT

12 x 1oz portions Camembert
2 eggs, beaten
1 cup dry bread crumbs
oil, for cooking
BLUEBERRY SAUCE:
2 teaspoons cornstarch
8oz blueberries, thawed if frozen
¼ cup sugar
2 teaspoons lemon juice
sprig of mint, to garnish

Freeze the Camembert portions for 1 hour. Dip each cheese portion in egg, then in bread crumbs. Dip portions again in egg and crumbs. Put on a plate; chill until needed.

To make blueberry sauce, in a saucepan blend cornstarch smoothly with ⅓ cup water. Add remaining ingredients and simmer until the liquid thickens, stirring all the time. Serve warm.

Heat oil in the fondue pot on top of the stove then transfer to the lighted spirit burner. The Camembert portions are cooked in hot oil at the table, using Chinese wire strainers if possible to lift them out of the pot (fondue forks will pierce the crust and cause cheese to ooze out). Serve with the sauce. Garnish with a sprig of mint.

Serves 6.

ALPINE TARTIFLETTE

butter, for greasing
12oz potatoes, scrubbed
2 tablespoons butter
1 small onion, chopped
4oz smoked bacon, cut into small pieces
1 Reblochon cheese
salt and freshly ground black pepper
5 tablespoons light cream
green salad, to serve

Preheat the oven to 425F (220C). Butter a gratin dish. Place scrubbed potatoes in a pan of cold water and bring to a boil.

Cook for 15-20 minutes until tender. Drain, and when cool enough to handle, peel, and cut into thick slices. Meanwhile, heat butter in a skillet. Add onion and cook for a few minutes until soft. Add bacon and cook until lightly browned. Remove onion and bacon with a slotted spoon, drain on paper towels, and set aside. Add potato slices to the pan and cook for 2-3 minutes on each side, until golden.

Cut the Reblochon in half and then into cubes, leaving the crust on. Make layers of potato, bacon, onion, and cheese, seasoning each layer with salt and pepper. Pour cream over the top, and cook in the oven for 10-12 minutes or until the top has browned. Serve with green salad.

Serves 2.

RACLETTE

2lb small new potatoes
salt and freshly ground black pepper
1lb Raclette cheese
TO SERVE:
air dried ham
salami
pickled gherkins

Scrub potatoes and place in a pan of cold salted water. Bring to a boil and cook for 10-15 minutes until tender. Drain and place in a warm serving bowl. Season with salt and pepper.

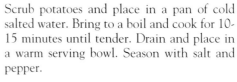

To cook the cheese, slice cheese thinly and place a layer of slices on a shallow metal tray and place under a hot broiler until it starts to melt. Scrape the top melted layer of cheese off with a palette knife.

Place melted cheese on top of potatoes. Continue to cook the remaining cheese in the same way. Serve with the ham, salami, and gherkins.

Serves 4.

CHEESE FONDUE TARTS

15oz puff pastry
1¾ cups grated Beaufort cheese
1¾ cups grated Jarlsberg cheese
1 clove garlic, crushed
⅔ cup light cream
1 tablespoon lemon juice
2 teaspoons cornstarch
3 tablespoons vodka
salt and freshly ground black pepper
2 tablespoons chopped fresh chives

Preheat the oven to 425F (220C). On a floured surface, roll the pastry out to ⅛ inch thick and cut out twelve 4 inch circles.

Place circles in a 12-cup muffin pan. Prick bottoms and chill for 10 minutes. Press foil into pastry cases and fill with dried beans. Bake for 15-20 minutes then remove foil and beans and bake for 5 more minutes until golden.

Meanwhile, put grated cheeses, garlic, cream, and lemon juice in a pan. Cook over a gentle heat, stirring, until smooth. In a small bowl combine cornstarch and vodka, add to cheese mixture, and cook for 2 minutes. Season with salt and pepper, and stir in chives. Divide cheese fondue between the pastry cases and serve at once.

Makes 12.

BAKED CAMEMBERT

1 small whole Camembert cheese in its box
2 cloves garlic
2 tablespoons dry white wine (optional)
chunks of crusty bread, to serve
BACON-WRAPPED POTATOES:
16 small new potatoes weighing about 1lb
salt
8 slices bacon
1 teaspoon Dijon mustard

Preheat the oven to 400F (200C). Prepare potatoes. Scrub them and place in a pan of salted water. Bring to a boil and boil for 10-15 minutes until tender. Drain.

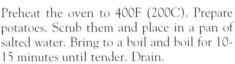

Meanwhile, remove wrapping around cheese. Peel garlic cloves and cut into slivers. Push garlic slivers into the surface of cheese. Drizzle wine over, if using, so that it soaks into the holes. Remove cheese from box and wrap in foil. Bake the cheese in the oven for 25-30 minutes until boiling.

Cut each bacon slice in half across. Stretch out slightly with the back of a knife and smear with a little mustard. Wrap a piece of bacon round each potato, and secure with a wooden toothpick. Broil potatoes, turning once, until bacon is brown and crisp. Remove foil from the cheese and serve in the box, with bacon-wrapped potatoes and crusty bread.

Serves 2-3.

FISH

CARIBBEAN FISH FONDUE

CRISPY COD BITES

2 teaspoons hot pepper sauce
2 teaspoons soft brown sugar
1 teaspoon crushed allspice
1 clove garlic, crushed
½ teaspoon ground coriander
juice 1 lime
1½lb cod loin
2½ cups coconut milk
1 Scotch bonnet chili
salt
MANGO SALSA:
1 mango, peeled and finely diced
½ small red onion, finely diced
1 fresh red chili, seeded and finely chopped
3 tablespoons chopped fresh cilantro
grated rind and juice 1 lime

1½lb thick cod fillet, skinned
seasoned flour, for dusting
2 eggs, beaten
2 cups fresh bread crumbs
oil, for cooking
LEMON PARSLEY SAUCE:
6 teaspoons butter
6 teaspoons all-purpose flour
1 cup fish stock
grated rind and juice ½ lemon
1 tablespoon chopped fresh parsley
salt and freshly ground black pepper
3 tablespoons light cream

Cut fish in bite-size pieces. Toss in flour, dip in egg, then coat in bread crumbs.

In a bowl, mix together hot pepper sauce, sugar, allspice, garlic, coriander, and lime juice. Cut fish into cubes and add to the bowl. Stir to coat in the marinade, cover, and leave in a cool place for 30 minutes. (See above.) Meanwhile, make the mango salsa. In a bowl, mix together mango, onion, chili, cilantro, and lime rind and juice. Set aside. Remove the fish from the marinade, drain, and arrange on a serving plate.

To make lemon parsley sauce, melt butter in a saucepan, stir in flour, and cook for 1 minute. Gradually add stock, then bring to a boil and simmer 1-2 minutes until sauce thickens, stirring all the time. Stir in lemon rind and juice, parsley, and season with salt and pepper. Reheat for 1 minute, then stir in cream.

Heat the coconut milk and Scotch bonnet chili in the fondue pot on top of the stove. Season with salt then transfer to the lighted spirit burner. Spear the fish on to the fondue forks and cook in the hot coconut milk for 2-3 minutes. Serve with the mango salsa.

Serves 4.

Heat the oil in the fondue pot on top of the stove then transfer to the lighted spirit burner. Spear the fish on to fondue forks and cook in the hot oil. Serve the fish with the sauce.

Serves 4-6.

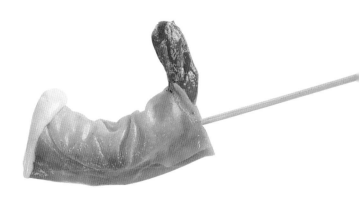

SEAFOOD KABOBS

8 large scallops
1¼lb monkfish, boned
seasoned flour, for dusting
oil, for cooking
TARRAGON WINE SAUCE:
6 teaspoons butter
1 shallot, finely chopped
⅔ cup dry white wine
2 teaspoons chopped fresh tarragon
salt and freshly ground black pepper
4 tablespoons light cream

Remove the coral parts from scallops and reserve. Cut white parts in half.

Cut monkfish into bite-size pieces. Toss scallops and monkfish in seasoned flour. Thread one piece of scallop and 2 pieces of monkfish on to 16 bamboo skewers and keep in refrigerator until needed. Heat the oil in the fondue pot on top of the stove then transfer to lighted spirit burner.

To make sauce, melt butter in a saucepan. Add shallot and cook until soft, then add reserved scallop corals and cook over a gentle heat for 5 minutes. Pour in wine, add tarragon, and season with salt and pepper. Simmer for 5 minutes. Purée sauce in a blender or food processor until smooth, then return to saucepan, stir in cream, and keep warm. Cook kabobs in hot oil until crisp and golden and serve with the sauce.

Serves 4.

SHRIMP IN JACKETS

2 sheets filo pastry approximately 18x10 inches
2 tablespoons butter, melted
9oz (approximately 32) large raw shrimp, peeled and
    thawed if frozen
salt and freshly ground black pepper
oil, for cooking
WASABI MAYONNAISE:
⅔ cup mayonnaise
1 teaspoon wasabi paste
2 teaspoons lime juice

Make the wasabi mayonnaise. In a bowl, mix together mayonnaise, wasabi paste, and lime juice. Set aside.

Lightly brush sheets of filo pastry with melted butter. Cut each sheet into strips across. The strips should be as wide as the shrimp are long. Cut each strip in half across. Dry shrimp on paper towels and season with salt and pepper. Roll a strip of pastry round each shrimp and arrange on a serving dish.

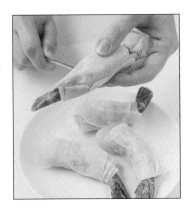

Heat the oil in the fondue pot on top of the stove then transfer to the lighted spirit burner. Spear the wrapped shrimp on the fondue forks and cook in the hot oil for 2 minutes or until crisp and golden. Serve with the wasabi mayonnaise.

Serves 4.

SEAFOOD FONDUE

8oz raw jumbo shrimp
2½ cups good fish stock
½ lemon, sliced
1 small onion, peeled
8oz monkfish, skinned
8oz thick cod fillet, skinned
8oz scallops
lemon wedges and parsley sprigs, to garnish
Rouille (see page 88), to serve

Peel the shrimp and place the shells in a saucepan with the stock, lemon, and onion. Bring to a boil and simmer for 10 minutes.

Cut monkfish and cod into cubes and halve the scallops if they are large. Arrange on serving plates with the peeled shrimp. Garnish with lemon wedges and parsley sprigs. Cover and keep cool.

Strain stock into the fondue pot, bring back to a boil on top of the stove, then transfer to the lighted spirit burner. Spear the fish on to the fondue forks and cook in the hot stock for 2-3 minutes. Serve with Rouille.

Serves 6.

VARIATION: The selection of fish can be varied according to personal preference and what is available.

SWEET & SOUR FISH FONDUE

2 eggs
1 cup all-purpose flour
1½lb boneless skinless firm white fish
   such as monkfish, cut into cubes
oil, for cooking
SWEET & SOUR SAUCE:
1 tablespoon oil
1 small onion, finely chopped
1 green bell pepper, seeded and sliced
1 teaspoon cornstarch
2 tablespoons soft brown sugar
2 tablespoons white wine vinegar
2 tablespoons tomato paste
juice 1 small orange
2 tablespoons soy sauce
2 tablespoons finely chopped pineapple

To make sauce, heat the oil in a saucepan. Add onion and cook for 5 minutes until beginning to soften. Add bell pepper and cook for 5 more minutes. In a small bowl, blend cornstarch with 4 tablespoons water and add to the pan with sugar, vinegar, tomato paste, orange juice, soy sauce, and pineapple. Bring to a boil, stirring, and cook until the sauce thickens. Keep warm.

Make the batter; whisk eggs with scant 1 cup iced water until frothy. Add flour and beat until just blended. Divide between 6 small bowls. Divide the fish between 6 serving plates. Heat oil in the fondue pot on top of the stove then transfer to the lighted spirit burner. Spear the fish on to the fondue forks, dip in the batter, then in hot oil for 2-3 minutes until batter is crisp and golden. Serve with the sweet and sour sauce.

Serves 6.

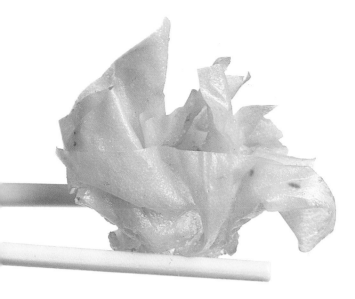

WAFER-WRAPPED SHRIMP

12oz peeled shrimp, coarsely chopped
1 fresh green chili, seeded and finely chopped
2 teaspoons oyster sauce
2 sheets filo pastry
oil, for cooking
CHILI SAUCE:
4 tablespoons tomato sauce
1-2 teaspoons chili sauce
1/2 teaspoon sesame oil

In a bowl, mix shrimip, chili, and oyster sauce together.

Cut filo pastry into 4 inch squares. Place a heaping teaspoon of shrimp filling in the center of each square, then draw the corners of the pastry together and twist them to form little bundles. Place on a floured serving plate. Cover and chill until required. (Do not make these too far in advance – as bases become soggy if left to stand for too long.) Heat the oil in the fondue pot on top of the stove then transfer to the lighted spirit burner.

To make chili sauce, put tomato sauce, chili sauce, 2 tablespoons water, and sesame oil into a saucepan and heat gently for 3-4 minutes. Cook bundles using small Chinese wire strainers – this makes it easier and safer when lifting bundles out of the hot oil. Serve the shrimp bundles with the hot chili sauce, as a starter.

Makes 24.

PIRI PIRI SHRIMP

1 fresh red chili, seeded and very finely chopped
1/2 teaspoon paprika
1/2 teaspoon ground coriander
1 clove garlic, crushed
finely grated rind 1 lime
salt and freshly ground black pepper
9oz large raw shrimp, peeled and thawed if frozen
oil, for cooking
lime wedges, to garnish
Aioli (see page 89) and bread, to serve

In a bowl, mix together chili, paprika, ground coriander, garlic, lime rind, salt, and pepper.

Add shrimp and mix well. Cover and leave in a cool place for 30 minutes. Heat the oil in the fondue pot on top of the stove then transfer to the lighted spirit burner.

Thread shrimp on to fondue forks or bamboo skewers and cook in the hot oil for 1 minute or until pink. Serve, garnished with lime wedges, with the aioli and bread.

Serves 4.

ANCHOVY & SHRIMP FONDUE

2oz anchovy fillets, drained
1 clove garlic, halved
⅔ cup dry white wine
1 cup grated Gruyère cheese
2 cups grated Cheddar cheese
1 teaspoon cornstarch
2 tablespoons dry sherry
Tabasco sauce
TO SERVE:
8oz large peeled cooked shrimp
cubes of French bread

Place anchovy fillets in a mortar and pound to a paste with the pestle. Arrange shrimp and bread on serving plates.

Rub inside of a fondue pot with cut clove of garlic. Pour in wine and heat gently on the stove until boiling. Gradually stir in both cheeses. Heat gently, stirring, until the cheese has melted. In a small bowl, blend cornstarch with the sherry.

Stir cornstarch mixture into cheese and add Tabasco sauce, to taste, and anchovy paste. Cook gently, stirring until thick and creamy. Transfer pot to the lighted spirit burner. Serve with the shrimp and bread.

Serves 4-6.

SPICY SHRIMP

1½lb cooked Mediterranean shrimp
2 tablespoons oil
1 teaspoon paprika
2 tablespoons lemon juice
oil, for cooking
PIQUANT SAUCE:
1¼ cups tomato juice
2 teaspoons soft brown sugar
2 teaspoons red wine vinegar
¼ teaspoon ground cinnamon
¼ teaeaspoon ground ginger
1 small fresh red chili, seeded and finely chopped

Peel shrimp, leaving tail shells on, if desired, and put into a bowl. Add oil, paprika, and lemon juice; mix well.

Cover shrimp and leave to marinate for at least 1 hour in refrigerator. To make piquant sauce, put all ingredients into a saucepan and simmer for 15 minutes. Keep warm.

Drain and arrange shrimp on a serving plate. Heat the oil in the fondue pot on top of the stove then transfer to the lighted spirit burner. Heat the shrimp in the hot oil and serve with hot piquant sauce.

Serves 6 as a starter, 4 as a main course.

Note: Raw Mediterranean shrimp may be used, if desired. Follow instructions given above, then cook raw shrimp in hot oil for 2-3 minutes.

BAGNA CAUDA

¼ cup butter
4 cloves garlic, crushed
2oz can anchovy fillets, drained and roughly chopped
⅔ cup mild extra virgin olive oil
TO SERVE:
a selection of raw and blanched vegetables such as
  celery, carrots, fennel, bell peppers, radishes,
  asparagus, cauliflower, baby artichoke hearts
hard boiled quails' eggs
breadsticks
toasted cubes of ciabatta bread

CRISPY CRUMBED MUSSELS

2¼lb fresh mussels in shells
2 lemons, quartered
6 cloves garlic, peeled
2 eggs, beaten
2 cups fresh bread crumbs
oil, for cooking
lemon wedges, to garnish
Rouille (see page 88), to serve

Arrange vegetables, eggs, and bread on serving plates.

Scrub mussels and remove the beards. Discard any which do not close when tapped sharply. Place mussels in a large pan with lemon quarters and garlic. Add 4 tablespoons water to the pan.

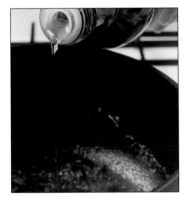

Gently heat butter in a heavy saucepan. Add garlic and cook gently, for 2 minutes. Add anchovies, then pour in oil very slowly, stirring constantly. Cook gently, stirring, for about 10 minutes. Do not allow to boil. The sauce in ready when anchovies have become a paste.

Cover and cook on a high heat for a few minutes, shaking pan occasionally until mussels open. Discard any which remain closed. Drain mussels and remove from shells. Dry on paper towels. Place beaten egg and bread crumbs in 2 separate shallow dishes. Dip the mussels into egg, allowing the excess to drip back, then dip in bread crumbs. Place on a serving dish.

Transfer sauce to an earthenware bagna cauda pot or a fondue pot and place over the lighted spirit burner. To serve, dip vegetables, eggs, and bread into the anchovy sauce.

Serves 4-6.

Heat the oil in the fondue pot on top of the stove then transfer to the lighted spirit burner. Thread the mussels, two at a time, on to fondue forks or bamboo skewers and cook in the hot oil for 1 minute or until crisp and golden. Serve, garnished with lemon wedges, with the rouille.

Serves 4.

VARIATION: For a quick version of this dish, ready prepared breaded mussels, squid, or scampi could be used.

THAI FISH CAKES

1lb boneless cod fillet
2 tablespoons chopped fresh cilantro
1 tablespoon Thai red curry paste
1 small egg, beaten
1 teaspoon soft brown sugar
1 tablespoon cornstarch
1 teaspoon salt
oil, for cooking
lime wedges, to garnish
CHILI DIPPING SAUCE:
4 tablespoons rice vinegar
4 tablespoons soy sauce
1 teaspoon soft brown sugar
1 clove garlic, crushed
1 fresh red chili, seeded and finely chopped
1 teaspoon sesame oil

Cut cod into chunks and chop roughly in a food processor. Add chopped cilantro, curry paste, egg, sugar, cornstarch, and salt. Process again until well blended. Chill the mixture for 30 minutes. Divide mixture into 16 pieces, roll each into a ball, then flatten slightly into a cake. Place on a serving dish and chill. (See above.) Make the dipping sauce. Place vinegar, soy sauce, sugar, garlic, chili, and sesame oil in a bowl and whisk together. Divide between small serving bowls.

Heat oil in the fondue pot on top of the stove then transfer to the lighted spirit burner. To cook the fishcakes, place them in wire baskets and dip into hot oil for 2-3 minutes until golden and cooked through. Serve, garnished with lime wedges, with the dipping sauce.

Serves 4.

SWORDFISH ACAPULCO

1½lb swordfish steaks, cut into bite-size pieces
MARINADE:
4 tablespoons oil
⅔ cup dry white wine
1 clove garlic, crushed
THOUSAND ISLAND SAUCE:
1 hard boiled egg
1 cup mayonnaise
1 teaspoon tomato paste
2 tablespoons chopped stuffed olives
2 tablespoons finely chopped onion
salt and freshly ground black pepper
1 tablespoon chopped fresh parsley

Combine marinade ingredients; stir in fish.

Cover and leave fish to marinate in refrigerator for 2-3 hours. To make Thousand Island sauce, chop hard boiled egg. Put all ingredients into a bowl, season to taste with salt and pepper, and mix together. Spoon into a serving dish.

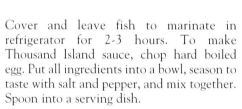

Drain the fish from the marinade and arrange in a serving dish. Heat the oil in the fondue pot on top of the stove then transfer to the lighted spirit burner. Cook the fish in the oil and serve with the Thousand Island sauce.

Serves 4.

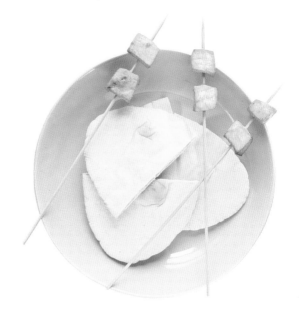

NIÇOISE FONDUE

1 tablespoon olive oil
1 onion, finely chopped
2 cloves garlic, crushed
14oz can chopped tomatoes
½ cup dry white wine
1 teaspoon dried herbes de Provence
3½oz canned or bottled anchovies, drained
2 tablespoons pitted olives, chopped
salt and freshly ground black pepper
12oz cooked French beans, halved
3 hard boiled eggs, quartered
4 tablespoons vinaigrette dressing
1lb fresh tuna fish
French bread, to serve

MARRAKESH SWORDFISH FONDUE

1 small red onion, finely chopped
2 cloves garlic, crushed
1 fresh red chili, seeded and finely chopped
2 tablespoons chopped fresh cilantro
1 tablespoon chopped fresh mint
1 teaspoon ground cumin
1 teaspoon paprika
pinch saffron strands
4 tablespoons olive oil
juice 1 lemon
salt
1½lb swordfish, skinned
oil, for cooking
green salad and warm pita bread, to serve

Heat the oil in a pan, add onion and garlic, and cook gently for 10 minutes or until soft. Add tomatoes, white wine, ⅓ cup water, and herbes de Provence and simmer gently for about 10 minutes until well blended. (See above.) Process in a blender or food processor to make a smooth sauce, then add anchovies and olives, and process briefly until finely chopped. Season with salt and pepper and pour into the fondue pot.

In a bowl, mix together the onion, garlic, chili, cilantro, mint, cumin, paprika, saffron, olive oil, lemon juice, and salt. (See above.) Cut monkfish into cubes. Add them to spice mixture in the bowl. Mix well to coat, cover, and leave in a cool place for 1 hour.

Combine beans and eggs with vinaigrette dressing and place in a serving dish. Cut tuna fish into cubes and arrange on a serving dish. Heat tomato sauce on top of the stove until simmering then transfer to the lighted spirit burner. Spear cubes of tuna fish on fondue forks and cook in the hot tomato sauce for 2 minutes or until cooked as desired. Serve with the bean and egg salad and French bread.

Serves 4.

Using a slotted spoon, remove fish from the bowl and arrange on a serving plate. Heat oil in the fondue pot on top of the stove then transfer to the lighted spirit burner. Spear fish on to the fondue forks and cook in the hot oil for 2-3 minutes. Serve with salad and warm pita bread.

Serves 4.

GEFILTE FISH

1½lb mixed white fish, skinned
1 small onion, quartered
1 egg, beaten
2 tablespoons chopped fresh parsley
¼ cup ground almonds
4 tablespoons fine matzo meal
salt and freshly ground black pepper
oil, for cooking
CREAMY BEET SAUCE:
⅔ cup thick sour cream
2oz cooked beet, grated
1 tablespoon horseradish sauce

Coarsely chop the fish and onion in a food processor.

Add the remaining ingredients except the oil to the fish and mix well. (The mixture should be stiff; if necessary add a little more matzo meal.) With wetted hands, form mixture into 36 smooth balls. Place on a tray and refrigerate for at least 30 minutes. Heat oil in the fondue pot on top of the stove then transfer to the lighted spirit burner.

To make creamy beet sauce, put cream into a bowl, add grated beet, then mix in horseradish sauce and season with salt and pepper. Cook the gefilte fish in the hot oil and serve with the sauce.

Serves 6.

SMOKED FISH GOUJONS

4 heaping tablespoons all-purpose flour
salt and freshly ground black pepper
1½lb skinless and boneless smoked fish fillets
3 eggs, beaten
2 cups fresh bread crumbs
oil, for cooking
lemon wedges, to garnish
REMOULADE SAUCE:
⅔ cup mayonnaise
1 teaspoon Dijon mustard
2 teaspoons finely chopped capers
2 teaspoons finely chopped gherkins
2 teaspoons finely chopped fresh tarragon

To make the sauce mix together the mayonnaise, mustard, capers, gherkins, and tarragon. Set aside. (See above.) Place flour in a shallow dish. Season with salt and pepper and mix together. Cut fish into strips about ½ inch wide. Dust strips with seasoned flour. Place beaten egg and bread crumbs in 2 separate shallow dishes. Dip each piece of fish in the egg allowing the excess to drip back in, then dip in bread crumbs. Place on a serving dish.

Heat oil in the fondue pot on top of the stove then transfer to the lighted spirit burner. Spear fish on to fondue forks and cook in oil for 1-2 minutes until crisp and golden. Serve, garnished with lemon wedges, with the sauce.

Serves 4.

AMANDINE TROUT

4 trout
seasoned flour, for dusting
2 eggs, beaten
2 cups blanched almonds, lightly toasted and finely
    chopped
oil, for cooking
DILL SAUCE:
4 teaspoons cornstarch
⅔ cup fish stock
⅔ cup milk
2 tablespoons chopped fresh dill
salt and freshly ground black pepper

Clean and bone the fish and cut off fins, then slice into pieces just under ½ inch thick.

Toss pieces of trout first in seasoned flour, then dip in egg and finally coat in chopped almonds. Place on a serving plate and refrigerate until ready to cook. Heat oil in the fondue pot on top of the stove then transfer to the lighted spirit burner.

To make dill sauce, in a saucepan blend cornstarch smoothly with a little fish stock, then add remainder together with the milk and heat until simmering, stirring all the time. Cook for 2 minutes until thickened. Stir in dill and season with salt and pepper. Cook the fish in the hot oil and serve with the hot dill sauce.

Serves 4.

FISH FIREPOT

1½lb assorted boneless skinless fish such as salmon,
    cod, and monkfish
8oz large raw peeled shrimp or scallops or a mixture
    of both
1lb pak choi, cut into thin strips
8oz button mushrooms, halved
7oz fine egg noodles, cooked
chopped fresh cilantro
7½ cups fish stock
3 tablespoons rice wine or dry sherry
1 teaspoon salt
DIPPING SAUCE:
1 fresh red chili, seeded and finely chopped
2 cloves garlic, crushed
4 tablespoons soy sauce
1 tablespoon tamarind paste

Cut fish into thin slices and halve scallops if they are large. (See above.) Arrange fish on 4 or 6 individual serving plates. Cover and chill until required. Arrange pak choi, mushrooms, and noodles on serving plates. Place chopped cilantro in a shallow dish. Make dipping sauce. In a bowl, mix together chili, garlic, soy sauce, and tamarind paste. If using a Mongolian hotpot, light it and place on the table. Pour in stock and add rice wine or sherry and salt. Bring to a boil.

(If using a fondue pot, pour stock and rice wine or sherry into the pot, add salt, and bring to a boil on the stove. Transfer to the lighted spirit burner.) Dip pieces of fish into stock, using chopsticks or Chinese wire strainers. Remove from stock and dip into sauce or cilantro before eating. From time to time add mushrooms and pak choi to the stock, and when cooked remove and eat. Finally, add noodles to stock to heat through, then serve the soup in warmed bowls.

Serves 6.

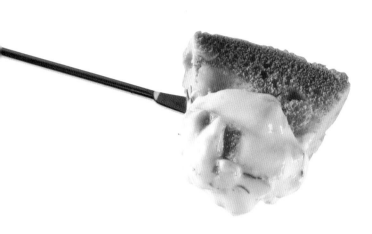

MANHATTAN FONDUE

8-10 bagels
4oz smoked salmon
1¼ cups cream cheese
¾ cup milk
1 tablespoon chopped fresh dill
salt and freshly ground black pepper

Split the bagels, toast lightly, and cut into bite-size pieces. Divide between 4-6 serving plates.

Chop smoked salmon into small pieces. Place cream cheese and milk in the fondue pot and heat gently on the stove until cheese has melted to a smooth sauce.

Stir in the dill and smoked salmon, and season with salt and a generous amount of black pepper. Transfer the pot to the lighted spirit burner and keep warm over a low heat. Spear the pieces of bagel on fondue forks and dip into the sauce.

Serves 4-6.

SEAFOOD TEMPURA

4 plaice fillets, skinned
8oz halibut, skinned and boned
8oz fresh salmon, skinned and boned
8oz scampi tails, thawed if frozen
4 small squid, cut into rings
1 quantity Chili Sauce (see page 31)
3 teaspoons peeled and grated fresh ginger root and
   8oz daikon, grated, to garnish
1 quantity Batter (see page 62)
oil, for cooking

Cut plaice, halibut, and salmon into thin slices or fingers; arrange on a platter with scampi and squid.

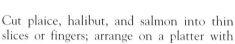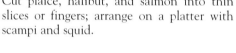

Make chili sauce. Prepare the garnish by mixing ginger and daikon together.

Make the batter. Heat oil in the fondue pot on top of the stove then transfer to the lighted spirit burner. Each person spears a piece of fish, dips it into the batter, then cooks it in the hot oil. The cooked food is then dipped into the chili sauce and eaten with the garnish.

Serves 4-6.

MEAT
& POULTRY

STEAK BOURGUIGNONNE

2¼lb lean fillet or rump steak
oil, for cooking
small baked potatoes and green salad, to serve
 (optional)
FOUR SAUCES:
2½ cups mayonnaise
2oz anchovies, drained
2 tablespoons horseradish sauce
2 tablespoons tomato paste
2 teaspoons hot pepper sauce
1 tablespoon curry paste

Cut steak into 1 inch cubes and arrange on
6 serving plates.

To make the sauces, divide mayonnaise
between 4 bowls. Using a mortar and pestle,
pound anchovies to a puree, and stir into one
of the bowls of mayonnaise. Stir horseradish
sauce into another, tomato paste and hot
pepper sauce into another, and curry paste
into the last bowl. Transfer sauces to small
serving bowls.

Heat oil in the fondue pot on top of the
stove then transfer to the lighted spirit
burner. Spear steak on to fondue forks and
cook in hot oil according to individual taste.
Serve with the sauces, and baked potatoes
and salad, if you like.

Serves 6.

VARIATIONS: Lean fillet of lamb could be
served instead of or as well as the steak.

MEXICAN FONDUE

2¼lb lean rump steak
oil, for cooking
MEXICAN SAUCE:
1 tablespoon oil
½ Spanish onion, finely chopped
1 clove garlic, crushed
14oz can tomatoes
2 tablespoons tomato paste
½ teaspoon chili powder
1 fresh green chili, seeded and finely chopped
salt and freshly ground black pepper

Cut meat into 1 inch cubes and arrange on a
serving plate.

To make Mexican sauce, heat oil in a
saucepan, add onion and garlic, and cook
gently until softened. Stir in tomatoes and
their juice, tomato paste, and chili powder.
Simmer, uncovered, for 10 minutes.

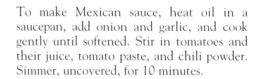

Remove sauce from heat and purée in a
blender or food processor until smooth, or
press through a sieve to give a smooth sauce.
Return to the heat, add chopped chili, and
simmer for a further 15 minutes. Season with
salt and pepper. Heat oil in the fondue pot
on top of the stove then transfer to the
lighted spirit burner. Cook the meat in the
hot oil and serve with the sauce.

Serves 4-6.

FONDUE BOURGUIGNONNE

2¼lb fillet steak
oil, for cooking
TOMATO SAUCE:
1 tablespoon oil
2 shallots, finely chopped
1 clove garlic, crushed
14oz can chopped tomatoes
2 tablespoons tomato paste
salt and freshly ground black pepper
1 tablespoon chopped fresh parsley

To make tomato sauce, heat oil in a saucepan, add shallots, and cook gently until soft.

Stir in garlic, tomatoes with their juice, and tomato paste. Season with salt and pepper, bring to a boil, then reduce heat and simmer, uncovered, for about 30 minutes or until sauce has reduced and thickened. Stir in parsley and serve hot or cold.

Cut the steak into 1 inch cubes and put into a serving dish. Heat oil in the fondue pot on top of the stove then transfer to the lighted spirit burner. Each person spears a cube of meat with a fondue fork and immerses the meat in the hot oil to fry. The meat cube is cooked according to individual taste.

Serves 4-6.

Note: Serve also with Garlic Sauce (see page 60) and Cool Curry Dip (see page 63).

CAJUN MEATBALLS

1 tablespoon oil
1 onion, finely chopped
1 teaspoon coriander seeds
½ teaspoon cardamom seeds
1lb lean ground steak
1 cup fresh bread crumbs
1 small egg, beaten
grated rind ½ lemon
¼-½ teaspoon chili powder
2 tablespoons chopped fresh cilantro
salt and freshly ground black pepper
oil, for cooking
TO SERVE:
Chili Tomato Sauce (see page 88)
pita bread
shredded lettuce

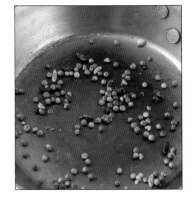

Heat oil in a saucepan. Add onion and cook for 10 minutes until soft. Set aside to cool. In a small heavy saucepan, dry fry coriander and cardamom seeds for a few minutes until golden, then crush, using a mortar and pestle. In a bowl, mix together the onion, ground steak, crushed spices, bread crumbs, egg, lemon rind, chili powder, cilantro, and salt and pepper until thoroughly combined.

Form the mixture into walnut-size balls. Arrange on serving plates and chill until required. Heat oil in the fondue pot on top of the stove then transfer to the lighted spirit burner. Spear meatballs on to the fondue forks and cook in the hot oil for 3-4 minutes until cooked. Serve with the sauce, pita bread and lettuce.

Serves 4-6.

PROVENÇAL BEEF

2 cloves garlic, crushed
⅔ cup red wine
grated rind and juice ½ orange
1 tablespoon chopped fresh rosemary
1 teaspoon dried herbes de provence
2 tablespoons olive oil
1¼lb rump or fillet steak
salt and freshly ground black pepper
oil, for cooking
TOMATO SALAD:
1lb tomatoes, sliced
6 scallions, thinly sliced
2 tablespoons shredded basil leaves
1 clove garlic, crushed
6 tablespoons olive oil
2 tablespoons balsamic vinegar

In a bowl, mix together garlic, wine, orange rind and juice, rosemary, herbes de provence, and olive oil. Cut steak into 1 inch cubes and add to marinade. Cover and marinate overnight in the refrigerator. Meanwhile, make salad. Arrange sliced tomatoes on individual serving plates. Sprinkle scallions and basil over tomatoes. In a small bowl, whisk together garlic, olive oil, balsamic vinegar, and salt and pepper. Pour over tomatoes, cover, and leave to marinate for 1 hour.

Remove steak from marinade and dry on paper towels. Season with salt and pepper and arrange on serving plates. Heat oil in the fondue pot on top of the stove then transfer to the lighted spirit burner. Spear the steak on to fondue forks and cook in hot oil for 3-4 minutes until cooked. Serve with the tomato salad.

Serves 4.

TERIYAKI FONDUE

2¼lb fillet steak
3 teaspoons light soft brown sugar
½ cup soy sauce
6 tablespoons dry sherry
2 cloves garlic, crushed
1 teaspoon ground ginger
oil, for cooking
BEAN SPROUT SALAD:
1 small head Chinese leaves
8oz fresh bean sprouts
1 red bell pepper, seeded and finely sliced
½ bunch scallions, shredded
6 tablespoons sunflower oil
1 tablespoon wine vinegar

Thinly cut steak into long narrow strips.

Put 1 teaspoon of sugar and 2 tablespoons of soy sauce into a bowl and set aside. In a large bowl, combine remaining sugar and soy sauce, sherry, garlic, and ginger. Add strips of meat and leave to marinate for 1 hour. Weave the strips of meat on to 20-24 bamboo skewers ready for cooking.

Heat oil in the fondue pot on top of the stove then transfer to the lighted spirit burner. To prepare the salad, shred Chinese leaves and put into a bowl with bean sprouts, bell pepper, and scallions. Add oil to reserved sugar and soy sauce, then whisk in vinegar and pour over salad. Toss lightly together. Cook the meat in hot oil and serve with the salad.

Serves 4-6.

TERIYAKI STEAK

1½lb fillet steak
2 inch piece fresh ginger root
1 tablespoon oil
1 clove garlic, crushed
4 tablespoons soy sauce
2 tablespoons mirin or medium sherry
1 teaspoon soft light brown sugar
freshly ground black pepper
TO SERVE:
1 daikon radish
2 tablespoons wasabi paste
cilantro sprigs

Cut the steaks into thin strips ½ inch wide and 4 inch long.

Peel ginger and grate into a bowl. Squeeze out liquid and put 1 tablespoon in a dish with oil, garlic, soy sauce, mirin or sherry, and sugar. Add steak, mix well, cover, and leave to marinate in the refrigerator for 1 hour. Meanwhile, prepare garnish. Peel daikon radish and grate into a bowl. Squeeze out as much liquid as possible and divide the grated daikon radish between 4 serving plates. Place a little wasabi paste and a sprig of cilantro on each plate.

Remove steak from marinade and pat dry with paper towels. Season with pepper. Thread strips of steak on to bamboo skewers and divide between 4 serving dishes. Heat oil in the fondue pot on top of the stove then transfer to the lighted spirit burner. Cook the steak in hot oil for 2-3 minutes until cooked. Serve with daikon radish and wasabi, garnished with cilantro.

Serves 4.

CHEESY MEATBALL FONDUE

1½lb lean ground beef
1 tablespoon finely chopped onion
½ cup fresh whole bread crumbs
salt and freshly ground black pepper
4oz Cheddar cheese, diced
oil, for cooking
TANGY SAUCE:
1 tablespoon tomato paste
1 tablespoon red wine vinegar
2 tablespoons honey
2 teaspoons dry mustard
1 tablespoon Worcestershire sauce
1¼cups chicken stock
2 teaspoons cornstarch
juice 1 orange

Mix together beef, onion, and bread crumbs. (See above.) Season meat mixture with salt and pepper and divide into 30 balls. Flatten each ball out, place a piece of cheese in center, then mold meat around cheese, sealing it well to enclose cheese completely.

To make sauce, put tomato paste, wine vinegar, honey, mustard, Worcestershire sauce, and stock into a saucepan and simmer for 10 minutes. Blend cornstarch smoothly with orange juice, then stir into the sauce and simmer for 1 minute, stirring all the time. Heat oil in the fondue pot on top of the stove then transfer to the lighted spirit burner. Cook meatballs in the hot oil and serve with the sauce.

Serves 6.

VEAL MILANESE

1½lb leg veal, cubed
3 tablespoons seasoned all-purpose flour
3 eggs, beaten
1 cup dry bread crumbs
2 teaspoons finely grated lemon rind
oil, for cooking
ITALIAN SAUCE:
2 tablespoons olive oil
1 onion, finely chopped
1-2 cloves garlic, crushed
1½lb ripe tomatoes, peeled and chopped
5 tablespoons dry white wine
salt and freshly ground black pepper
1 tablespoon chopped fresh basil

Toss veal in flour; dip in egg and coat in mixed crumbs and lemon rind. (See above.) To make Italian sauce, heat oil in a saucepan, add onion and garlic, and cook over a low heat until soft. Add tomatoes and wine, and season with salt and pepper. Simmer for 30 minutes. Purée sauce in a blender or food processor until smooth, or press through a sieve.

Heat oil in the fondue pot on top of the stove then transfer to the lighted spirit burner. Stir basil into sauce and reheat sauce. Cook meat in hot and oil and serve with sauce.

Serves 4-6.

Note: Serve also with Lemon Parsley Sauce (see page 28), omitting fish stock and using chicken stock instead.

MEXICAN BEEF & GUACAMOLE

1½lb sirloin or rump steak
2 teaspoons chili sauce
2 cloves garlic, crushed
1 tablespoon chopped fresh cilantro
1 teaspoon each dried oregano and ground cumin
juice 1 lime
oil, for cooking
tortilla chips, to serve
GUACAMOLE:
2-3 ripe avocados, depending on the size
½ red onion, finely chopped
1 tablespoon chopped fresh cilantro
1 clove garlic, crushed
1 red chili, seeded and finely chopped
2 tomatoes, peeled, seeded, and finely chopped
juice ½-1 lime
pinch sugar
salt and freshly ground black pepper

Cut steak into 1 inch cubes. In a bowl, mix together chili sauce, garlic, cilantro, oregano, cumin, and lime juice. Add steak and mix well. (See above.) Cover and marinate in the refrigerator for 1-2 hours. Meanwhile, make guacamole. Peel and pit avocados, place in a bowl, and mash with a fork. Do not make mixture too smooth. Stir in onion, cilantro, garlic, chili, and tomato. Then stir in lime juice, sugar, and salt and pepper to taste.

Leave to stand for 30 minutes, but no longer than 1 hour. Just before serving, stir again and transfer to small serving bowls. Remove steak from marinade, dry with paper towels, and arrange on serving plates. Heat oil in the fondue pot on top of the stove then transfer to the lighted spirit burner. Spear cubes of steak on to fondue forks and cook in hot oil for 3-4 minutes until cooked. Serve with guacamole and tortilla chips.

Serves 4-6.

KOFTAS & RAITA

1 small onion, roughly chopped
1 clove garlic, chopped
1 inch piece fresh ginger root, peeled and chopped
1 teaspoon ground cumin
1 teaspoon ground coriander
1 tablespoon oil
1lb lean ground lamb
3 tablespoons chopped fresh cilantro
salt and freshly ground black pepper
1 small egg, beaten
oil, for cooking
naan bread or chapatis, to serve
RAITA:
½ cucumber
1½ cups Greek-style yogurt
3 tablespoons chopped fresh mint

PROVENÇAL MEATBALLS

1½lb ground beef
1 small onion, finely chopped
2oz stuffed olives, finely chopped
1 small egg, beaten
salt and freshly ground black pepper
all-purpose flour, for coating
oil, for cooking
PROVENÇAL DIP:
1 eggplant, diced
3 tablespoons olive oil
1 shallot, finely chopped
1 clove garlic, crushed
1lb tomatoes, peeled and chopped
1 tablespoon tomato paste
1 tablespoon chopped fresh parsley

Put onion, garlic, and ginger in a blender or food processor and chop finely, without turning to a paste. Add cumin and ground coriander, and process briefly to blend. Heat oil in a skillet, add onion mixture, and cook for 2-3 minutes, stirring. (See above.) Leave to cool. In a bowl, mix together ground lamb, cilantro, seasoning, and cooled onion mixture. Mix thoroughly. Add just enough beaten egg to bind mixture together. With floured hands, roll mixture into bite-size balls. Arrange on serving plates and chill until required.

Sprinkle eggplant for dip with salt and drain for 30 minutes. In a bowl, mix together ingredients for meatballs, except flour. With wetted hands, roll mixture into 36 small balls, then coat in flour. Chill in refrigerator until needed.

To make the raita, grate cucumber coarsely. Squeeze out as much liquid as possible then mix cucumber, yogurt, and mint together. Season with salt and pepper, and transfer to small serving bowls. Heat oil in the fondue pot on top of the stove then transfer to the lighted spirit burner. Spear the koftas on to fondue forks and cook in the hot oil for 3-4 minutes until cooked. Serve with the raita and naan bread or chapatis.

Serves 4-6.

To make dip, rinse eggplant and pat dry. Heat oil in a large saucepan and cook shallot and garlic gently for 2 minutes. Add eggplant and cook gently for 10 minutes. Add tomatoes and tomato paste, cover, and cook for a further 5-8 minutes until vegetables are almost reduced to a pulp. Stir in parsley and seasoning. Heat oil in the fondue pot on top of the stove then transfer to the lighted spirit burner. Cook the meatballs in oil and serve with the warm dip.

Serves 6.

MIDDLE EASTERN FONDUE

1½lb lean leg of lamb, cubed
MARINADE:
3 tablespoons olive oil
1 tablespoon lemon juice
1 clove garlic, crushed
1 tablespoon chopped fresh mint
1 teaspoon ground cinnamon
salt and freshly ground black pepper
APRICOT SAUCE:
1 tablespoon oil
1 shallot, finely chopped
14oz can apricots in natural juice
1 tablespoon chopped fresh parsley

Mix marinade ingredients together and pour over cubed lamb.

Cover lamb mixture and leave to marinate for at least 2 hours, or preferably overnight. To make apricot sauce, heat oil in a saucepan, add shallot, and cook over a low heat until soft. Add apricots and their juice, and simmer for 5 minutes.

Purée sauce in a blender or food processor, then season with salt and pepper and stir in parsley. Reheat before serving. Remove lamb from marinade and arrange on a serving plate. Heat the oil in the fondue pot on top of the stove then transfer to the lighted spirit burner. Cook the lamb in the oil and serve with the sauce.

Serves 4.

TURKISH LAMB

1½lb lean lamb
2 cloves garlic, crushed
4 tablespoons lemon juice
pinch chili powder
1 teaspoon ground cumin
1 teaspoon ground coriander
½ teaspoon ground cinnamon
salt and freshly ground black pepper
oil, for cooking
TO SERVE:
Tomato and Olive Salsa (see page 90)
pita bread

Cut the lamb into 1 inch cubes.

Crush garlic and place in a bowl. Add lemon juice, chili powder, cumin, ground coriander, and cinnamon, and stir. Add lamb and mix until well coated with marinade. Cover and leave to marinate in a cool place for 2 hours.

Remove lamb from marinade and pat dry with paper towels. Season with salt and pepper. Arrange the lamb on 4 serving plates. Heat the oil in the fondue pot on top of the stove then transfer to the lighted spirit burner. Spear the lamb on to fondue forks and cook in the hot oil for 3-4 minutes until cooked. Serve with the tomato and olive salsa.

Serves 4.

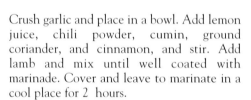

GROUND LAMB FONDUE

1¼lb ground lean lamb
3 scallions, finely chopped
1 cup fresh bread crumbs
2 tablespoons chopped fresh parsley
salt and freshly ground black pepper
oil, for cooking
MUSHROOM SAUCE:
¼ cup butter
6oz mushrooms, finely chopped
6 teaspoons all-purpose flour
1¼ cups milk
1 tablespoon dry sherry

Put the ingredients for lamb balls into a bowl.
Season with salt and pepper and mix well.

With wetted hands, shape mixture into 20-
24 balls, the size of a walnut, and place on a
serving plate. Heat the oil in the fondue pot
on top of the stove then transfer to the
lighted spirit burner.

To make sauce, melt butter in a saucepan,
add mushrooms, and cook gently for
5 minutes. Stir in flour, then slowly add milk
and bring to a boil, stirring. Simmer for a
further 5 minutes, then season with salt and
pepper and add sherry. Cook the lamb balls
in the hot oil and serve with the warm sauce.

Serves 4-6.

Note: Serve also with Deviled Sauce (see
right).

BACON PARCELS

12oz bacon, rinds removed
8oz chicken livers
oil, for cooking
DEVILED SAUCE:
3 teaspoons butter
1 shallot, finely chopped
3 teaspoons all-purpose flour
⅔ cup chicken stock
4 tomatoes, peeled and chopped
1 tablespoon tomato paste
2 teaspoons sugar
1 tablespoon red wine vinegar
3 teaspoons Worcestershire sauce
½ teaspoon paprika
pinch cayenne pepper

Cut bacon slices in half; cut livers into
pieces. (See above.) Wrap bacon around
chicken livers and spear on to bamboo
skewers. Place on a serving plate. Heat the
oil in the fondue pot on top of the stove then
transfer to the lighted spirit burner.

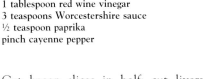

To make deviled sauce, melt butter in a
saucepan, add shallot, and cook until soft.
Stir in flour, then add stock and remaining
ingredients. Simmer for 15 minutes, then
strain sauce. Cook the bacon parcels in the
hot oil and serve with the hot sauce.

Serves 4.

Note: Serve also with Creamy Onion Sauce
(see page 62).

PORK SATAY

1 teaspoon tamarind paste
2 cloves garlic, crushed
2 tablespoons soy sauce
1 teaspoon ground cumin
1 teaspoon ground coriander
½ teaspoon chili powder
salt
1lb lean pork steaks
oil, for cooking
SATAY SAUCE:
2 tablespoons smooth peanut butter
scant 1 cup coconut cream
2 teaspoons red Thai curry paste
1 tablespoon fish sauce
1 tablespoon soft brown sugar

In a bowl mix together tamarind paste, garlic, soy sauce, ground cumin, ground coriander, chili, and salt. (See above.) Place pork steaks between 2 pieces of plastic wrap and beat out flat with a meat hammer or rolling pin. Cut into strips then place in the bowl with marinade. Mix well then cover and leave in a cool place for 1 hour. Remove from marinade, dry with paper towels, and thread on to bamboo skewers. Arrange on serving plates.

To make satay sauce, place peanut butter, coconut cream, red curry paste, fish sauce, and brown sugar in a pan. Heat gently to form a smooth sauce, adding a little water if necessary. Keep warm. Heat oil in the fondue pot on top of the stove then transfer to the lighted spirit burner. Cook the skewers of pork in the hot oil for 3-4 minutes until cooked. Serve with the satay sauce.

Serves 4.

CRISPY SAUSAGE BITES

1lb pork sausage
1 small onion, finely chopped
⅓ cup cream cheese
1 tablespoon chopped fresh parsley
1 teaspoon prepared mustard
½ cup fresh bread crumbs
salt and freshly ground black pepper
2 eggs, beaten
¾ cup dry bread crumbs
oil, for cooking
RELISH SAUCE:
Tomato Sauce (see page 41)
2 tablespoons sweet pickle relish

Put sausage and onion into a skillet; cook until lightly brown and crumbly.

Turn into a bowl and add cream cheese, parsley, mustard, fresh bread crumbs, and season with salt and pepper. Shape into 16-20 small firm balls, molding to make them smooth. Dip first in beaten egg, then roll in dry bread crumbs until evenly coated. Chill until required.

To make relish sauce, put tomato sauce in a saucepan, stir in relish, and heat through. Keep warm. Heat oil in the fondue pot on top of the stove then transfer to the lighted spirit burner. Each person spears a sausage ball with a fondue fork and immerses it in the hot oil to fry until crisp and golden. Serve with the warm sauce.

Serves 4.

PORK & PEANUT SAUCE

½ teaspoon chili powder
1 teaspoon ground coriander
½ teaspoon turmeric
3 teaspoons oil
3 teaspoons soy sauce
½ teaspoon salt
2¼lb pork fillet, cubed
oil, for cooking
PEANUT SAUCE:
⅔ cup desiccated coconut
1¼ cups boiling water
5 tablespoons crunchy peanut butter
2 teaspoons sugar
1 fresh green chili, seeded and finely chopped
1 teaspoon lemon juice
1 clove garlic, crushed

In a bowl, mix together spices, oil, soy sauce, and salt to make a paste. Add pork and, with wet hands, knead paste into meat. Cover bowl and leave in the refrigerator for at least 2 hours.

To make peanut sauce, put coconut into a bowl, pour boiling water over, and leave to stand for 15 minutes. Strain mixture into a saucepan, pressing well to extract all moisture. Discard coconut. Add remaining ingredients and mix well. Cook over a low heat, stirring until the sauce comes to a boil. Heat oil in the fondue pot on top of the stove then transfer to the lighted spirit burner. Cook the meat in hot oil and serve with the hot sauce.

Serves 4-6.

FIVE-SPICE DUCK

3-4 duck breasts, about 1½lb total weight
1 teaspoon sesame oil
3 tablespoons soy sauce
3 tablespoons rice wine or dry sherry
1 tablespoon honey
1 tablespoon lime juice
2 teaspoons five-spice powder
1 clove garlic, crushed
1 inch piece fresh ginger root, grated
lime wedges, to garnish
oil, for cooking
TO SERVE:
shredded scallions
shredded celery
hoisin or plum sauce
Chinese pancakes or flour tortillas

Remove skin and fat from duck breast halves and cut meat into thin strips. Place in a shallow dish. In a bowl, mix together sesame oil, soy sauce, rice wine or sherry, honey, lime juice, five-spice powder, garlic, and ginger. (See above.) Pour over duck and stir well. Cover and leave in a cool place to marinate for 30 minutes. Remove duck strips from marinade and dry on paper towels. Arrange on serving plates and garnish with lime wedges. Arrange scallions and celery on serving plates and place hoisin or plum sauce in small bowls.

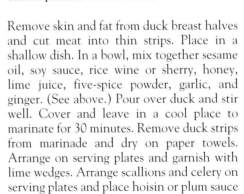

Warm Chinese pancakes or tortillas and keep warm. Heat oil in the fondue pot on top of the stove then transfer to the lighted spirit burner. Spear strips of duck on to fondue forks, or thread on to bamboo skewers. Cook in hot oil for 3-4 minutes until cooked. To serve, spread a little hoisin or plum sauce on a pancake or tortilla, add some scallion and celery, and place a few strips of cooked duck on top then roll up.

Serves 4-6.

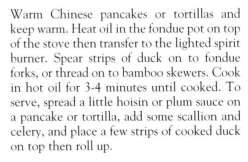

FRUITY DUCK FONDUE

1½lb duck breast fillets, cut in pieces
6 teaspoons seasoned flour
1 teaspoon five-spice powder
oil, for cooking
MARMALADE SAUCE:
1 tablespoon soft brown sugar
⅔ cup orange juice
4 tablespoons mature orange marmalade
juice 1 lemon
⅓ cup raisins, chopped if large
WINE AND CHERRY SAUCE:
1 tablespoon sugar
12oz can black cherries, drained
⅓ cup red wine
pinch mixed spice

CURRIED APRICOT TURKEY

1 tablespoon oil
1 onion, finely chopped
1 clove garlic, crushed
2 bay leaves
juice 1 lemon
2 tablespoons curry powder
4 tablespoons apricot jam
4 tablespoons apple juice
salt
1½lb turkey fillet
4 tablespoons crème fraîche
oil, for cooking

Heat oil in a saucepan. Add onion, garlic, and bay leaves and cook for 10 minutes until soft.

Toss duck in flour and five-spice powder. (See above.) Place duck on a serving plate. To make marmalade sauce, put all the ingredients into a small saucepan and simmer for 5 minutes. Keep warm.

Add lemon juice, curry powder, apricot jam, apple juice, and salt to taste. Cook gently for 5 minutes. Transfer to a bowl and leave to cool. Cut turkey into 1 inch cubes and add to cooled marinade. Mix well, cover and leave to marinate in the refrigerator for 2 hours.

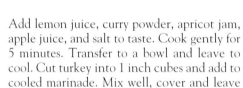

To make wine and cherry sauce. Put all ingredients into a saucepan and simmer for 15 minutes. Press through a sieve, discarding the pits. Keep warm. Heat oil in the fondue pot on top of the stove then transfer to the lighted spirit burner. Cook the duck in the hot oil and serve with the warm sauces.

Serves 4.

Remove turkey and allow marinade to run back into the bowl. Dry turkey with paper towels and arrange on 4 serving plates. Transfer marinade to a pan and simmer for 2 minutes. Stir in crème fraîche. Heat oil in the fondue pot on top of the stove then transfer to the lighted spirit burner. Spear turkey on to fondue forks and cook in hot oil for 3-4 minutes until cooked. Serve with the sauce.

Serves 4.

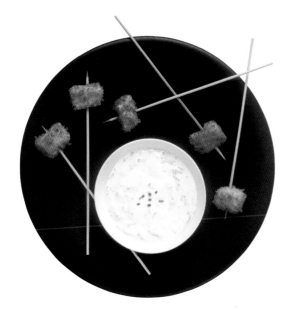

TURKEY NUGGETS

1½lb turkey fillets
3 tablespoons all-purpose flour
salt and freshly ground black pepper
1 cup dry bread crumbs
2 teaspoons finely grated lemon rind
2 extra large eggs, beaten
lemon wedges, to garnish
oil, for frying
HERB DIP:
1 cup fromage frais
1 clove garlic, crushed
2 tablespoons chopped fresh tarragon
1 tablespoon chopped fresh chives
1 tablespoon chopped fresh chervil
salt and freshly ground black pepper

Cut turkey into bite-size cubes. In a bowl, mix together flour, salt, and pepper. In a shallow dish, mix together bread crumbs and lemon rind. Pour beaten egg into another shallow dish. Toss turkey cubes in seasoned flour, dip in beaten egg, then coat in bread crumbs. (See above.) Arrange on serving plates and garnish with lemon wedges. To make herb dip, place fromage frais in a bowl, add garlic, tarragon, chives, and chervil, and season with salt and pepper. Mix well together then divide between small serving bowls.

Heat oil in the fondue pot on top of the stove then transfer to the lighted spirit burner. Spear turkey nuggets on to fondue forks and cook in hot oil for 3-4 minutes until cooked. Serve with the herb dip.

Serves 4-6.

VARIATION: Chicken may be used as an alternative to turkey.

SPICY CHICKEN FONDUE

6 skinless, boneless chicken breast halves
4 tablespoons oil
2 teaspoons paprika
½ teaspoon chili powder
oil, for cooking
CURRY SAUCE:
1 tablespoon oil
1 onion, finely chopped
2 teaspoons mild curry powder
3 teaspoons all-purpose flour
1¼ cups milk
6 teaspoons mango chutney
salt and freshly ground black pepper

Cut chicken into ¾ inch pieces and mix with oil, paprika, and chili powder.

Place chicken on a serving plate. To make curry sauce, heat oil in a saucepan, add onion, and cook until soft. Stir in curry powder and cook for 2 minutes, then stir in flour.

Gradually stir in milk and bring slowly to a boil, stirring all the time. Continue to cook until sauce thickens. Simmer for 5 minutes, then add chutney and season with salt and pepper. Heat oil in the fondue pot on top of the stove then transfer to the lighted spirit burner. Cook the chicken in the hot oil and serve with the hot sauce.

Serves 4-6.

TURKEY CRANBERRY DIP

1½ cups sugar
1lb fresh cranberries
2 tablespoons port
2¼lb cooked, diced turkey or chicken

In a large saucepan, put sugar and scant 2 cups water. Heat gently, stirring to dissolve sugar, then boil for 5 minutes.

Add cranberries and simmer for about 10 minutes until skins pop.

Remove from heat and stir in port. Pour mixture into fondue pot. Serve with diced turkey or chicken for dipping.

Serves 6.

HARISSA-SPICED CHICKEN

2 teaspoons coriander seeds
1½ teaspoons cumin seeds
2 cloves garlic
1-2 tablespoons chili paste
½ teaspoon salt
4 tablespoons olive oil
1½lb skinless, boneless chicken breast
oil, for cooking
Couscous Salad (see page 91), to serve
TOMATO & PRESERVED LEMON SALSA:
3-4 ripe tomatoes
½ preserved lemon
2 scallions, chopped
2 tablespoons liquid from the preserved lemons
1 tablespoon chopped fresh mint
salt and freshly ground black pepper

Heat a heavy skillet. Add coriander and cumin seeds, and dry fry, stirring, for 2 or 3 minutes until they give off a fragrant aroma. (See above.) Grind to a powder using a mortar and pestle. Place ground seeds in a bowl with garlic, chili paste, salt, and olive oil. Mix together. Cut chicken into cubes and add to marinade. Cover and leave in the refrigerator for 1 hour. Make the salsa. Cut tomatoes into dice and place in a bowl. Remove flesh from preserved lemon and cut skin into dice.

Add to tomatoes with scallions, preserved lemon liquid, mint, and salt and pepper. Transfer to small serving bowls. Remove chicken from marinade and dry with paper towels. Arrange on serving plates. Heat oil in the fondue pot on top of the stove then transfer to the lighted spirit burner. Spear chicken on to fondue forks and cook in hot oil for 3-4 minutes. Serve with the salsa and couscous salad.

Serves 4.

CHICKEN TIKKA

2 inch piece fresh ginger root
4 tablespoons plain yogurt
1-2 tablespoons hot Madras curry paste
2 cloves garlic, crushed
1 teaspoon turmeric
2 tablespoons lemon juice
1 teaspoon paprika
½ teaspoon salt
1½lb skinless, boneless chicken breast
cilantro sprigs and lemon wedges, to garnish
oil, for cooking
TO SERVE:
Raita (see page 45)
naan bread
poppadoms

JERK CHICKEN

grated rind and juice 1 lime
1 inch piece fresh ginger root
3 tablespoons olive oil
1 clove garlic, crushed
1 teaspoon dried thyme
1 teaspoon ground cinnamon
1 teaspoon ground allspice
1 teaspoon soft brown sugar
2 teaspoons hot pepper sauce
salt and freshly ground black pepper
2lb skinless, boneless chicken breast
lime wedges, to garnish
oil, for frying
Bean Salad (see page 94), to serve

Peel ginger and grate into a bowl. Add the yogurt, curry paste, garlic, turmeric, lemon juice, paprika, and salt. Mix together thoroughly. (See above.) Cut chicken into ¾ inch cubes. Add to marinade and mix well. Cover and leave in the refrigerator to marinate for at least 2 hours. Remove from marinade and allow as much of the marinade to drain off as possible.

Grate rind from lime and squeeze juice into a bowl. Peel ginger and grate into the bowl. Add olive oil, garlic, thyme, cinnamon, allspice, sugar, hot pepper sauce, and salt and pepper. Mix together. (See above.) Cut chicken into 1 inch cubes and add to marinade. Cover and leave in a cool place to marinate for 2 hours.

Thread chicken cubes, 2 or 3 together, on to bamboo skewers and arrange on serving plates, garnished with cilantro and lemon wedges. Heat oil in the fondue pot on top of the stove then transfer to the lighted spirit burner. Cook chicken in hot oil for 3-4 minutes until cooked. Serve with the raita, naan bread, and poppadoms.

Serves 4.

Remove chicken from marinade, pat dry with paper towels, and arrange on serving plates. Garnish with lime wedges. Heat oil in the fondue pot on top of the stove then transfer to the lighted spirit burner. Spear chicken on to fondue forks and cook in hot oil for 3-4 minutes until cooked. Serve with the salad.

Serves 6.

CHICKEN GOUJONS

1½lb skinless, boneless chicken breast
seasoned flour, for dusting
3 eggs, beaten
¾ cup dry bread crumbs
oil, for cooking
RED BELL PEPPER SAUCE:
6 teaspoons butter
1 small onion, chopped
2 red bell peppers, seeded and chopped
1 clove garlic, crushed
1 cup chicken stock
salt and freshly ground black pepper
sprig of dill, to garnish

Cut chicken in long strips about ½ inch wide.

Dust with seasoned flour, dip in egg, then coat with bread crumbs. Place in refrigerator to chill. To make red bell pepper sauce, in a small saucepan melt butter, add onion, and cook until soft. Add red bell peppers and garlic, and continue to cook over a gentle heat for 5 minutes. Pour in stock and simmer for 10 minutes or until bell peppers are tender.

Sieve red bell pepper sauce, season with salt and pepper, and reheat. Heat oil in the fondue pot on top of the stove then transfer to the lighted spirit burner. Cook chicken goujons in the hot oil. Garnish sauce with sprig of dill and serve hot with the goujons.

Serves 6.

THAI CHICKEN HOTPOT

2lb boneless chicken breast
12 button mushrooms
12 scallions, cut into 2 inch lengths
1 red bell pepper, seeded and cut into strips
4oz baby corn
4oz snow peas
1 bunch watercress
4oz fine egg noodles, broken into pieces
3¾ cups good chicken stock
2 small red chilies
3 kaffir lime leaves
1 stalk lemon grass, crushed
2 slices fresh galangal or ginger
1 carrot, cut into thin matchsticks
6 Chinese leaves, shredded
Thai Dipping Sauce (see page 55), to serve

Cut chicken into thin strips, place on 6 serving plates, cover, and chill until required. Divide mushrooms, scallions, bell pepper, corn, snow peas, and watercress between 6 plates, cover, and chill until required. Soak the egg noodles in boiling water for 3-4 minutes, then drain and transfer to a serving bowl. (See above.) Place stock in a saucepan or fondue pot. Add chilies, lime leaves, lemon grass, and galangal or ginger. Bring to a boil and simmer gently for 10 minutes. Add carrot.

Either transfer stock to a hot pot or transfer the fondue pot to the spirit burner. Using chopsticks or Chinese wire strainers, cook chicken and vegetables in the stock then dip in the dipping sauce to eat. When this is completed, add noodles and Chinese leaves, and ladle noodle soup into warmed bowls.

Serves 6-8.

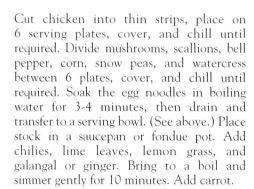

THAI CHICKEN MEATBALLS

1lb ground chicken
4 scallions, chopped
2 tablespoons chopped fresh cilantro
2 tablespoons Thai green curry paste
1 teaspoon soft brown sugar
1 teaspoon salt
lime wedges, to garnish
oil, for cooking
THAI DIPPING SAUCE:
1 fresh red chili, seeded and finely chopped
2 tablespoons light soy sauce
1 tablespoon Thai fish sauce
1 tablespoon lime juice
2 tablespoons soft brown sugar

SAVORY PARCELS

¼ cup butter
2 shallots, finely chopped
6oz bacon, chopped
1lb chicken livers, trimmed and chopped
8oz mushrooms, chopped
8 tablespoons chicken stock
2 egg yolks
pinch mixed dried herbs
salt and freshly ground black pepper
3-4 sheets filo pastry
1 egg white
oil, for cooking

Melt the butter in a large skillet, add the shallots, and cook for 2 minutes.

In a bowl, mix together chicken, scallions, cilantro, curry paste, sugar, and salt. (See above.) Form into small balls. Cover and chill for 30 minutes. Make the dipping sauce. Place chili, soy sauce, fish sauce, lime juice, and sugar in a bowl and mix together. Divide between 4 small dip dishes.

Add bacon and cook for 3-4 minutes. Stir in chicken livers and cook for 3 minutes, then add mushrooms and cook for 3 minutes. Pour stock into pan and simmer until it has almost evaporated. Cool slightly, then stir in egg yolks, herbs, and season with salt and pepper. Put mixture in a blender or food processor and chop coarsely. Leave to cool.

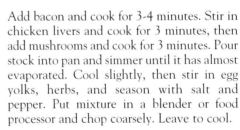

Arrange chicken balls on serving plates and garnish with lime wedges. Heat oil in the fondue pot on top of the stove then transfer to the lighted spirit burner. Spear chicken balls on to fondue forks and cook in hot oil for 3-4 minutes. Serve with the dipping sauce.

Serves 4.

Cut pastry into 18-24 x 6 inch squares. Place a tablespoon of chicken liver mixture at one end of each square. Fold over each side, then roll up parcel so it resembles a spring roll. Seal the edges with egg white, then set aside until needed. Heat oil in the fondue pot on top of the stove then transfer to the lighted spirit burner. Cook parcels in hot oil, using Chinese wire strainers for cooking and lifting them from hot oil.

Serves 6.

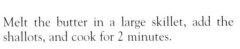

MONGOLIAN HOTPOT

3lb lean lamb, leg or fillet
7½ cups chicken stock
1 teaspoon peeled, grated fresh ginger root
1 clove garlic, crushed
2 tablespoons chopped scallion
2 tablespoons chopped fresh cilantro
4oz spinach leaves, shredded
8oz Chinese leaves, shredded
3oz instant soup noodles
HOTPOT DIPPING SAUCE:
6 tablespoons soy sauce
3 tablespoons smooth peanut butter
2 tablespoons rice wine or dry sherry
pinch chili powder
3 tablespoons hot water

Slice lamb very thinly and arrange on two large plates. Put stock into a large saucepan with ginger and garlic, and simmer for 15 minutes. Put scallion, cilantro, spinach, Chinese leaves, and noodles into separate serving bowls. Combine the ingredients for dipping sauce and divide between 6 small dishes.

Put stock into a special Mongolian hotpot or a fondue pot. Add scallions and bring back to a boil. Transfer pot to burner. Each person uses a fondue fork, or Chinese wire strainer, to cook pieces of food in stock. The food is then dipped in sauce before eating. Any remaining spinach and Chinese leaves are finally added to the pot with cilantro and noodles. When noodles are tender the soup is served in bowls.

Serves 6.

CANTONESE HOTPOT

8oz rump steak, fat removed
12oz skinless, boneless chicken breast
4oz snow peas
8oz peeled shrimp
1 red bell pepper, seeded and cut into strips
4oz button mushrooms, halved
8oz can bamboo shoots, drained
7½ cups chicken stock
2 teaspoons peeled, chopped fresh ginger root
2oz fine egg noodles
YELLOW BEAN SAUCE:
1 tablespoon soy sauce
2 tablespoons yellow bean sauce
1 tablespoon dry sherry
1 fresh green chili, seeded and finely chopped

Slice steak and chicken thinly and arrange on 6 individual plates. Top and tail snow peas and arrange on plates with shrimp and remaining vegetables. Put stock into a large saucepan with ginger and simmer for 15 minutes. Soak egg noodles in warm water for 10 minutes, then drain and put into a serving bowl. In a bowl, combine ingredients for yellow bean sauce, then add 2 tablespoons water and divide between 6 small dishes.

Pour stock into fondue pot, bring back to simmering; place over burner. Each person uses a fondue fork, or Chinese wire strainer, to cook pieces of food in stock. The cooked food is then dipped in sauce before eating. When all the meat and vegetables have been eaten, add noodles to fondue pot to heat through, then ladle soup into bowls.

Serves 6.

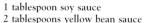

VEGETABLES

CAULIFLOWER CHEESE

1 cauliflower
crisp fried onions, to garnish
CHEESE SAUCE:
1 tablespoon butter
2 shallots, finely chopped
2 tablespoons all-purpose flour
1½ cups milk
½ cup grated Cheddar cheese
¼ cup grated Parmesan cheese
1 teaspoon Dijon mustard
pinch cayenne pepper
salt

Cut cauliflower into flowerets. Bring a pan of salted water to a boil.

Add cauliflower and boil for 5 minutes or until just tender. Drain thoroughly and divide between 4 serving plates. To make the cheese sauce, place butter in a saucepan and heat gently until melted. Add shallots and cook for 5 minutes until soft. Stir in flour and cook for 1 minute. Remove the pan from the heat and gradually stir in milk. Return the pan to the heat and bring to a boil then simmer gently, stirring for 2 minutes.

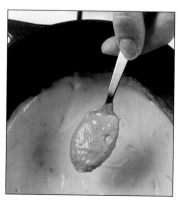

Stir in Cheddar cheese, Parmesan cheese, mustard, and cayenne pepper. Season with salt. Transfer the fondue pot to the lighted spirit burner. Scatter fried onions over the top. Spear the cauliflower flowerets on to fondue forks and dip into the sauce.

Serves 4.

FALAFEL FONDUE

1 cup dried chickpeas, soaked overnight in cold
  water and drained
2 tablespoons chopped fresh parsley
1 tablespoon chopped fresh cilantro
1 tablespoon tahini paste
1 clove garlic, crushed
1 tablespoon lemon juice
salt and freshly ground black pepper
seasoned flour, for dusting
oil, for frying
warm pita bread, to serve
CHILI YOGURT DIP:
⅔ cup Greek-style yogurt
1 fresh red chili, seeded and finely chopped
2 tablespoons chopped fresh cilantro

Process chickpeas in a blender or food processor until as smooth as possible. Transfer to a bowl and stir in parsley, cilantro, tahini, garlic, lemon juice, and salt and pepper. (See above.) Cover and set aside for 30 minutes. To make the chili dip, in a bowl, mix together the yogurt, chili, cilantro, salt, and pepper. Transfer to a serving bowl and set aside.

With floured hands, roll the chickpea mixture into 1 inch balls. Dust with seasoned flour. Arrange on serving plates. Heat oil in the fondue pot on top of the stove then transfer to the lighted spirit burner. Spear the falafel on to fondue forks and cook in the hot oil for 2 minutes or until evenly browned. Serve with the chili yogurt dip and warm pita bread.

Serves 4.

CAULIFLOWER FRITTERS

1 cauliflower, cut into flowerets
¾ cup dry bread crumbs
⅓ cup grated Parmesan cheese
1 tablespoon chopped fresh parsley
salt and freshly ground black pepper
2-3 eggs, beaten
oil, for cooking
CHEDDAR CHEESE SAUCE:
3 teaspoons butter
6 teaspoons all-purpose flour
1¼ cups milk
½ teaspoon prepared mustard
½ cup grated Cheddar cheese
pinch cayenne pepper

SPRING ROLLS

1 tablespoon oil
1 teaspoon sesame oil
1 clove garlic, crushed
1 fresh red chili, seeded and finely sliced
1lb pack fresh stir-fry vegetables
½ inch piece fresh ginger root, grated
1 tablespoon dry sherry or rice wine
1 tablespoon soy sauce
salt and freshly ground black pepper
12 spring roll wrappers
1 small egg, beaten
lime wedges and fresh cilantro, to garnish
oil, for frying
Ginger Dipping Sauce (see page 64), to serve

Heat oils in a wok. Add garlic and chili.

Parboil cauliflower in a saucepan of boiling salted water for 4-5 minutes; drain well. (See above.) In a bowl, mix together bread crumbs, Parmesan cheese, and parsley, and season with salt and pepper. Dip cauliflower flowerets in beaten egg, then coat in bread crumb mixture. Put on to a serving plate and set aside until ready to cook.

Stir-fry for 30 seconds. Add vegetables and ginger and stir-fry for 1 minute more, then drizzle sherry or rice wine and soy sauce over. Allow mixture to bubble up for 1 minute. Season with salt and pepper. Using a slotted spoon, transfer the vegetables to a dish. Set aside until cool. Soften the spring roll wrappers, following the directions on the package. Place a spoonful of filling on a wrapper.

To make cheese sauce, melt butter in a small saucepan, stir in flour, and cook for 1 minute. Remove from heat and add milk slowly. Bring to a boil, stirring, then simmer for 2 minutes. Stir in mustard, cheese, cayenne, and season with salt and pepper. Keep hot. Heat oil in the fondue pot on top of the stove then transfer to the lighted spirit burner. Cook the cauliflower in the oil and serve with the hot sauce.

Fold over front edge and sides and roll up neatly, sealing edges with a little beaten egg. Repeat with remaining wrappers and filling. Divide spring rolls between 4 serving plates. Garnish with lime wedges and cilantro. Heat oil in the fondue pot on top of the stove then transfer to the lighted spirit burner. Dip rolls into oil, using fondue forks or Chinese wire baskets. Cook for 2 minutes or until crisp. Serve with the dipping sauce.

Serves 4-6.

Serves 4.

ONION BHAJI FONDUE

4 tablespoons gram flour
½ teaspoon turmeric
½ teaspoon ground cumin
½ teaspoon ground coriander
1 teaspoon garam masala
pinch cayenne pepper
1 egg, beaten
1 large onion, quartered and very thinly sliced
1 tablespoon chopped fresh cilantro
oil, for frying
MINTED YOGURT DIP:
1 cup Greek-style natural yogurt
1 clove garlic, crushed
3 tablespoons chopped fresh mint
salt and freshly ground black pepper

To make the dip, in a bowl mix together yogurt, garlic, mint, salt, and pepper. (See above.) Transfer to serving bowls and set aside. Put the gram flour, turmeric, cumin, coriander, garam masala, and cayenne pepper in a bowl and mix together. Stir in egg, season with salt and pepper, then add sliced onion and chopped cilantro. Heat the oil in the fondue pot on top of the stove then transfer to the lighted spirit burner.

To cook the bhajis, push teaspoonsful of mixture into oil with another spoon. Cook a few at a time for 2-3 minutes until crisp and golden. Remove from oil with Chinese wire nets. Serve with the yogurt dip.

Serves 4 as an appetizer.

SWISS POTATOES

2lb small new potatoes, scrubbed
2 eggs, beaten
1 cup herb stuffing mix
oil, for cooking
GARLIC SAUCE:
2 cups fresh white bread crumbs
2 cloves garlic
salt and freshly ground black pepper
1 cup olive oil
4 teaspoons lemon juice
1 tablespoon white wine vinegar

Boil potatoes in skins until just tender; drain and cool. Dip in beaten egg, then roll in stuffing mix and set aside.

To make garlic sauce, dampen bread crumbs with 1 tablespoon water. Put into a blender or food processor with garlic and ½ teaspoon salt, and blend together until well mixed. Add oil a little at a time and continue to process until all the oil has been added.

Work the lemon juice and vinegar into the sauce until if forms a smooth, creamy consistency. Season with pepper. Turn mixture into a bowl. Heat the oil in the fondue pot on top of the stove then transfer to the lighted spirit burner. Spear the potatoes and cook in the hot oil; serve with the sauce.

Serves 4-6.

Note: Serve the potatoes also with Cheddar Cheese Sauce (see page 59).

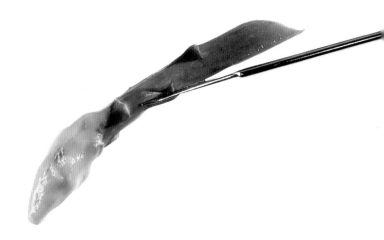

SPICY CHICKPEA BALLS

¾ cup bulgar wheat
½ cup boiling water
1¼ cups chickpeas, soaked overnight
2 tablespoons sunflower oil
2 cloves garlic, crushed
½ teaspoon baking powder
1 teaspoon chili powder
1 teaspoon each ground coriander and ground cumin
salt and freshly ground black pepper
oil, for cooking
FRESH TOMATO SAUCE:
4 tomatoes, peeled
½ green bell pepper, halved and seeded
½ red bell pepper, halved and seeded
1 fresh green chili, cored and seeded
1 tablespoon fresh coriander, chopped

Put the bulgar wheat into a bowl, pour the boiling water over, and leave the wheat to soak for 1 hour. Drain chickpeas and put into a food processor with bulgar wheat and remaining ingredients (except cooking oil and those for sauce). Blend for a few minutes until mixture becomes fairly smooth. With your hands, mold the mixture into 36 small balls and place on a serving dish.

To make the fresh tomato sauce, put all the ingredients into a blender or food processor and process until vegetables are finely chopped. Add seasoning, then put into a serving bowl. Heat the oil in the fondue pot on top of the stove then transfer to the lighted spirit burner. Spear the chickpea balls and cook in the hot oil. Serve with the fresh tomato sauce.

Serves 4-6.

ASPARAGUS FONDUE

15oz canned asparagus spears
1 clove garlic, halved
1 cup dry white wine
12oz Edam cheese, grated
1 tablespoon cornstarch
4 tablespoons crème fraîche
salt and freshly ground black pepper
TO SERVE:
blanched fresh asparagus spears, cooked baby
  artichoke hearts, cubes of French bread

Drain asparagus and process in a blender or food processor until smooth. Set aside.

Rub the inside of the fondue pot with garlic, then pour in wine and heat until boiling. Gradually stir in cheese and cook, stirring, over a low heat, until cheese has melted. Blend together cornstarch and crème fraîche and stir into cheese mixture. Continue to cook for a few more minutes until thick and smooth.

Stir in asparagus purée and season with salt and pepper. Cook for another minute until heated through. Transfer the pot to the lighted burner. Serve with the asparagus spears, artichoke hearts, and bread.

Serves 4-6.

PUMPKIN FONDUE

4 small pumpkins or squash, the size of a grapefruit
10oz creamy blue cheese such as Dolcelatte
1 cup heavy cream
4 tablespoons fresh white bread crumbs
2 teaspoons chopped fresh sage
salt and freshly ground black pepper
HERB BREADSTICKS:
1lb package ciabatta bread mix
1 tablespoon dried oregano
1 tablespoon caraway seeds
oil, for brushing
flour, for dusting

Preheat the oven to 450F (230C). To make breadsticks, follow package instructions to after first rising of dough.

Turn dough on to a floured board, add oregano and caraway seeds, and knead again. Roll out to approximately ¼ inch thickness and slice into ¾ inch lengths. Brush a baking sheet with oil. Arrange breadsticks on baking sheet and leave in a warm place for about 10 minutes to rise. Dust with flour and bake for 15 minutes or until browned. Leave to cool and set aside. Reduce the oven temperature to 375F (190C). Slice the tops off pumpkins and scoop out the seeds and fibers.

Crumble half the cheese into pumpkins; top with half the cream. Scatter 1 tablespoon of bread crumbs in each pumpkin then top with remaining cheese and cream. Scatter sage over and season with salt and pepper. Replace tops on pumpkins then place in an ovenproof dish. Bake for 45 minutes or until cheese is boiling and pumpkins are soft. Serve with breadsticks to dip in then scrape out pumpkin flesh with a spoon.

Serves 4.

MIXED VEGETABLE KABOBS

4 zucchini, cut into slices
16 button mushrooms
1 red bell pepper, seeded and cut into chunks
1 green bell pepper, seeded and cut into chunks
oil, for cooking
CREAMY ONION SAUCE:
½ cup low fat soft cheese
⅔ cup plain yogurt
½ bunch scallions, finely chopped
BATTER:
2 extra large eggs
1 cup all-purpose flour

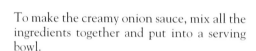

Thread the vegetables on to 12-16 bamboo skewers.

To make the creamy onion sauce, mix all the ingredients together and put into a serving bowl.

Make batter. Put eggs into a bowl with scant 1 cup iced water and beat until frothy. Add flour and beat until just blended – do not worry if a few lumps are left. Pour into a bowl and stand it in a larger bowl of ice. Heat the oil in the fondue pot on top of the stove then transfer to the lighted spirit burner. To cook kabobs, each person dips a skewer into the batter, then into hot oil to cook until the batter is golden. The kabobs are then eaten with the onion sauce.

Serves 4.

EGGPLANT FRITTERS

1lb eggplants, diced
1-2 teaspoons salt
seasoned flour, for dusting
oil, for cooking
BATTER:
1 cup all-purpose flour
2 eggs, separated
2 tablespoons olive oil
COOL CURRY DIP:
2 teaspoons curry paste
1 teaspoon Dijon mustard
2 teaspoons soft brown sugar
4 teaspoons grated onion
6 tablespoons mayonnaise
6 tablespoons plain yogurt

CHEESE & TOMATO FONDUE

2 cups canned tomato purée
scant 1 cup cream cheese
sugar, to taste
few drops Tabasco sauce
salt and freshly ground black pepper
frankfurters and cubes of ham, to serve
CORNMEAL MUFFINS:
½ cup self rising flour
1½ teaspoons baking powder
salt and freshly ground black pepper
1 cup fine cornmeal
½ cup grated Cheddar cheese
2 tablespoons butter, melted
1 extra large egg, beaten
⅔ cup milk

Put eggplant in a colander, add salt. (See above.) Leave eggplant to stand for 30 minutes. To make batter, sift flour and ¼ teaspoon salt into a bowl, beat in egg yolks and oil. Gradually add ¾ cup water and continue to beat to make a smooth batter. Leave to stand for 1 hour. Just before serving, whisk egg whites until stiff and fold into batter.

Preheat the oven to 400F (200C) Line 12 mini muffin pans with paper mini muffin cases. To make the muffins, sift flour, baking powder, salt, and pepper into a bowl then stir in cornmeal and cheese. (See above.) In a bowl, mix together butter, egg, and milk. Pour on to the dry ingredients and mix quickly until just combined. Do not overmix. Spoon the batter into prepared muffin cases. Bake for 10-15 minutes until well risen and golden brown. Leave to cool. Arrange on serving plates with the frankfurters and ham.

To make cool curry dip, whisk all ingredients together in a bowl, then spoon into a serving dish. Rinse eggplant under cold, running water and dry thoroughly on paper towels. Dust diced eggplant with seasoned flour. Heat the oil in the fondue pot on top of the stove then transfer to the lighted spirit burner. To cook fritters, each piece of eggplant is dipped into batter, then cooked in hot oil in the fondue pot.

Serves 4.

Place tomato purée and cream cheese in a fondue pot and heat gently until cheese has melted. Add sugar, Tabasco sauce, salt, and pepper to taste. Heat until just below simmering point then transfer to the fondue burner. Serve with the corn muffins, frankfurters, and ham for dipping.

Serves 4-6.

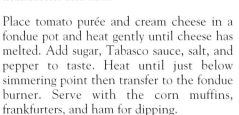

TEMPURA

oil, for frying
1lb assorted vegetables, such as red bell pepper
  strips, eggplant and zucchini batons, scallions,
  mushrooms, snow peas, baby corn, asparagus
BATTER:
1 cup all-purpose flour
1 egg, separated
1 teaspoon olive oil
salt and freshly ground black pepper
GINGER DIPPING SAUCE:
2 teaspoons each sesame oil, red wine vinegar, and
  soy sauce
3 tablespoons ginger syrup (from jar of ginger)
2 tablespoons honey
4 scallions, finely sliced

To make the batter, sift flour into a bowl. Measure 1 cup iced water into a pitcher and whisk in egg yolk and olive oil. Season with salt and pepper. Make a well in the middle of flour and gradually whisk in liquid. (See above.) Cover and stand for 1 hour. To make the dipping sauce, mix together the sesame oil, red wine vinegar, soy sauce, ginger syrup, and honey. Transfer to small dishes and sprinkle the scallions on top.

Whisk egg white until stiff then fold into the batter. Heat oil in the fondue pot on top of the stove then transfer to the lighted spirit burner. To serve, dip vegetables into batter, then into hot oil for 1-2 minutes until crisp and browned. Alternatively, spear two or three pieces of vegetables on to skewers and cook in the hot oil. Serve with the dipping sauce.

Serves 4.

AVOCADO FONDUE

2 avocados
1 tablespoon lime juice
1 clove garlic
1 cup dry white wine
12oz Gruyère cheese, grated
1 tablespoon cornstarch
salt and freshly ground black pepper
4 tablespoons sour cream
TO SERVE:
pickled jalapeño chilies, slices of apple, breadsticks,
  large peeled shrimp

Halve avocados and remove stones. Using a teaspoon, scoop out flesh and place in a bowl. Scrape out all bright green flesh next to skin.

Mash avocado until smooth then stir in lime juice. Cut garlic in half and rub round inside of the fondue pot. Pour in wine and heat until boiling. In a bowl, toss together cheese and cornstarch then stir into the wine. Cook gently, stirring, until cheese has melted.

Add avocado and cook, stirring, until smooth and heated through. Season with salt and pepper then stir in sour cream. Transfer the pot to the lighted burner and serve with the chilies, apple, breadsticks, and shrimp for dipping.

Serves 4-6.

WILD MUSHROOM FONDUE

¼oz dried wild mushrooms
3 tablespoons olive oil
4 shallots, finely chopped
2 cloves garlic, crushed
4oz fresh mixed wild mushrooms, chopped
3 tablespoons all-purpose flour
1 cup dry cider
12oz Emmental cheese, grated
4oz Roquefort cheese, crumbled
1 tablespoon chopped fresh tarragon
2 tablespoons light cream
TO SERVE:
cubes of ham, cherry tomatoes, cooked asparagus spears, and cubes of bread

Place dried mushrooms in a bowl and cover with boiling water. Leave to soak for 20 minutes. Drain, reserving ½ cup of soaking liquid. Chop soaked mushrooms finely. (See above.) In the fondue pot, heat the oil. Add shallots and garlic and cook for 5 minutes until soft. Add dried and fresh mushrooms and cook for a further 4-5 minutes until soft. Stir in flour and cook for 2 minutes. Gradually stir in reserved soaking liquid, then add cider.

Cook gently, stirring, until the mixture thickens then gradually stir in Emmental and Roquefort cheeses. Add the tarragon and continue to cook gently, stirring until the cheese is melted and the mixture is smooth and creamy. Stir in cream. Transfer pot to the lighted burner and serve with the ham, vegetables, and bread to dip in.

Serves 6.

BLACK-EYED PEA DIP

1 cup black-eyed peas, soaked overnight in cold water
1 clove garlic
few sprigs parsley
½ teaspoon salt
¼ cup butter
1 onion, chopped
1 teaspoon curry paste
⅔ cup plain yogurt
CURRIED BREAD CUBES:
1 small white loaf
vegetable oil, for frying
3 teaspoons curry powder

Drain soaking water from black-eyed peas.

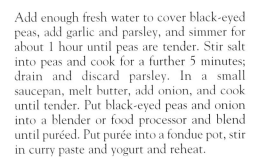

Add enough fresh water to cover black-eyed peas, add garlic and parsley, and simmer for about 1 hour until peas are tender. Stir salt into peas and cook for a further 5 minutes; drain and discard parsley. In a small saucepan, melt butter, add onion, and cook until tender. Put black-eyed peas and onion into a blender or food processor and blend until puréed. Put purée into a fondue pot, stir in curry paste and yogurt and reheat.

To make curried bread cubes, cut crusts off loaf, then cut bread into cubes. Heat oil in a skillet and fry bread until crisp and golden, then drain on paper towels. Sprinkle with curry powder and toss together. To eat, spear bread cubes with fondue forks and dip into bean fondue.

Serves 4-6.

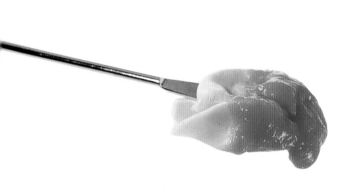

BELL PEPPER & TOMATO FONDUE

6 large tomatoes
4 red bell peppers
5 tablespoons olive oil
1 clove garlic, chopped
salt and freshly ground black pepper
1 onion, finely chopped
⅔ cup vegetable or chicken stock
2 tablespoons cornstarch, blended with a little water
fresh ravioli, cooked, to serve

Preheat the oven to 350F (190C). Oil 2 roasting pans. Cut tomatoes in half and cut red bell peppers into quarters and remove the seeds.

Place tomatoes, cut side up, in one of the roasting pans. Drizzle with 2 tablespoons of the olive oil and scatter with garlic. Season with salt and pepper. Place peppers in the other pan and drizzle with 2 tablespoons olive oil. Put tomatoes and peppers in the oven and roast tomatoes for 45-60 minutes until beginning to blacken round the edges. Cook the peppers, turning occasionally, until their skins are charred and blistered. Put in a plastic bag, seal, and leave until cool enough to handle, then peel and chop coarsely.

Heat remaining oil in a pan. Cook onion, stirring occasionally, for 5-10 minutes, until soft. Add peppers and stock. Cover and simmer for 15 minutes. Transfer to a blender or food processor, add tomatoes, and process until smooth. Press through a sieve and pour into the fondue pot. Heat on the stove until almost simmering. Stir cornstarch into mixture. Simmer for a few minutes until thickened then transfer to the lighted fondue burner. Serve with the ravioli.

Serves 4.

LEEK PURÉE

2lb leeks, coarsely chopped
⅔ cup chicken stock
¼ cup butter
salt and freshly ground black pepper
pinch freshly grated nutmeg
2 scallions, finely chopped
raw cauliflower flowerets, carrot sticks, and button mushrooms, to serve

Wash the leeks well, then put into a saucepan with 1 tablespoon water and cook for 10-15 minutes until soft.

Drain leeks and leave to cool slightly. Purée leeks in a blender of food processor with stock until smooth.

Spoon purée into fondue pot. Place over a gentle heat and beat in butter and season with salt, pepper and nutmeg. Stir in scallions and keep warm on a lighted spirit burner. Serve with a selection of raw vegetables or as an accompaniment to broiled meat.

Serves 4-6.

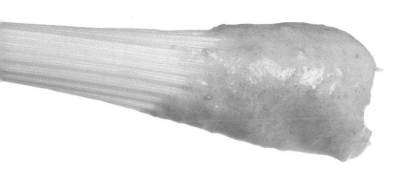

TOMATO NIÇOISE

¼ cup butter
1½lb ripe tomatoes
1 clove garlic, crushed
1 small onion, chopped
6oz canned pimentoes, drained and chopped
salt and freshly ground black pepper
pinch sugar
2 tablespoons mayonnaise
cooked artichoke leaves, cooked green beans,
  cucumber and celery sticks, to serve

Melt butter in a saucepan, add tomatoes,
garlic, onion, and pimento, and cook gently
for 10-15 minutes until soft.

Sieve mixture into a bowl; season with salt,
pepper, and sugar, and leave to cool. Whisk
in mayonnaise.

Pour the tomato Niçoise into a serving bowl.
To serve, arrange the vegetables on a large
platter and stand the bowl in the center.

Serves 4-6.

MUSHROOM FONDUE

¼ cup butter
1lb mushrooms, finely chopped
2 cloves garlic, crushed
⅔ cup chicken stock
⅔ cup heavy cream
3 teaspoons cornstarch
salt and freshly ground black pepper
pinch cayenne pepper
cubes of cheese and garlic sausage, to serve

Melt butter in a saucepan, add mushrooms
and garlic, and cook gently for 10 minutes.

Add stock and simmer for 10 minutes. Cool
slightly and purée in a blender or food
processor.

Put a little cream into the fondue pot, blend
in cornstarch smoothly, then add remaining
cream and the mushroom purée. Heat to a
simmer and cook over a gentle heat until
thickened, stirring frequently. Season with
salt, pepper, and cayenne. Serve with cubes
of cheese and garlic sausage.

Serves 4-6.

CORN FONDUE

1lb frozen corn kernels
2 teaspoons cornstarch
3 tablespoons light cream
salt and freshly ground black pepper
few drops Tabasco sauce
6 teaspoons butter
selection of cooked shrimp and mussels, to serve

Put corn into a saucepan with 2 tablespoons water and simmer for a few minutes until tender.

Drain the corn and put into a blender or food processor and process until soft but not too smooth. In a saucepan, blend cornstarch smoothly with cream. Add corn mixture and cook over a low heat until smooth.

Pour mixture into fondue pot, season with salt, pepper, and Tabasco sauce, then beat in butter. Set pot over a low burner to keep warm. Serve with a selection of cooked shellfish.

Serves 4-6.

THAI CORN FONDUE

14oz canned corn
1¼ cups chicken stock
scant 1 cup coconut cream
1 tablespoon Thai green curry paste
1 tablespoon Thai fish sauce
2 tablespoons cornstarch
2 tablespoons chopped fresh cilantro
TO SERVE:
blanched baby corn and snow peas
mini poppadoms
cooked peeled shrimp

Drain corn. In a blender or food processor, process corn to a purée and transfer to the fondue pot.

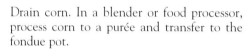
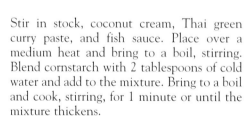

Stir in stock, coconut cream, Thai green curry paste, and fish sauce. Place over a medium heat and bring to a boil, stirring. Blend cornstarch with 2 tablespoons of cold water and add to the mixture. Bring to a boil and cook, stirring, for 1 minute or until the mixture thickens.

Stir in the chopped cilantro. Transfer the pot to the lighted fondue burner and serve with the baby corn, snow peas, poppadoms, and shrimp.

Serves 4.

Note: Vary the amount of Thai green curry sauce according to taste. For children, add a little less and for those who prefer a more fiery flavor, add more.

DESSERTS

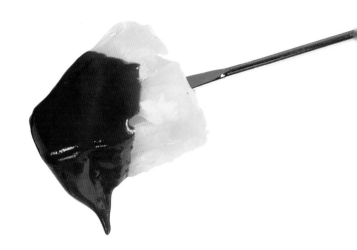

CLASSIC CHOCOLATE FONDUE

9oz dark chocolate
⅔ cup heavy cream
2 tablespoons brandy
selection of fruit such as strawberries, pineapple,
  banana, ground cherries, figs, and kiwi fruit, to
  serve
LADYFINGERS:
1½oz superfine sugar
1 egg
½ cup all-purpose flour, sifted

Preheat the oven to 375C (190C) Line a baking sheet with non-stick parchment. To make ladyfingers, place superfine sugar and egg in a large bowl.

Set bowl over a pan of barely simmering water and whisk together until thick and mousse-like. (See above.) Remove bowl from heat and gently fold in flour. Using a pastry bag fitted with a ½ inch plain tube, pipe finger lengths of mixture on to the prepared baking sheet. Bake for 6-8 minutes until golden. Transfer ladyfingers to a wire rack to cool.

Break up chocolate and place in the fondue pot with cream and brandy. Heat gently, stirring, until chocolate has melted and mixture is smooth. Transfer fondue pot to the lighted spirit burner and serve with the ladyfingers and fruit.

Serves 4-6.

VARIATION: For children, substitute orange juice for brandy.

CARIBBEAN CHOCOLATE FONDUE

1 pineapple
1 mango
2 bananas
juice ½ lime
13oz good-quality dark chocolate
scant 1 cup cream of coconut
2 tablespoons white rum
½ teaspoon freshly grated nutmeg

Cut the leafy top and the bottom off pineapple. Cut away skin and cut pineapple into quarters, lengthwise. Cut out core and cut each quarter into cubes.

Peel mango then cut down on either side of pit to remove flesh. Cut into cubes. Cut bananas into slices and sprinkle with lime juice.

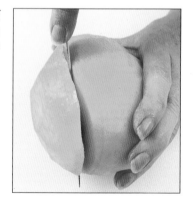

Break up chocolate into a fondue pot. Add cream of coconut and heat gently on the stove, stirring, until chocolate melts. Stir in rum and nutmeg, then place over a lighted spirit burner to keep warm. Serve with the fruit.

Serves 6.

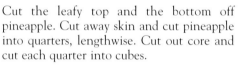

CHOCOLATE & HONEY FONDUE

10oz dark chocolate
1 generous tablespoon honey
1¼ cups heavy cream
SPICED FRUIT:
14oz ready-to-eat dried fruit such as apricots
  and prunes
1 cinnamon stick
1 star anise
4 cloves
1 tablespoon honey

To prepare the fruit, place in a saucepan and cover with water. Add cinnamon stick, star anise, and cloves, and bring to a boil.

Stir in honey and remove from the heat. Set aside and leave until cold. Drain fruit and pat dry on paper towels. Arrange on 6 individual plates.

Break up the chocolate and place in the fondue pot with honey and cream. Heat gently, stirring, until chocolate has melted and mixture is smooth. Transfer the fondue pot to the lighted spirit burner and serve with the fruit.

Serves 6.

Note: For both the fondue and fruit, choose a fragrant blossom honey such as Mexican wildflower honey.

MOCHA TIA MARIA FONDUE

8oz dark chocolate
3 teaspoons instant coffee powder
⅔ cup heavy cream
3 tablespoons Tia Maria
selection of fresh fruit, to serve
NUTTY MERINGUE:
2 egg whites
½ cup superfine sugar
2oz flaked almonds, lightly toasted

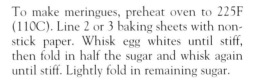

To make meringues, preheat oven to 225F (110C). Line 2 or 3 baking sheets with non-stick paper. Whisk egg whites until stiff, then fold in half the sugar and whisk again until stiff. Lightly fold in remaining sugar.

Put teaspoonfuls of mixture on to lined baking sheets to make a total of 30. Insert a few almonds into each one, then bake for 1½-2 hours until dry and crisp. Turn off oven, but leave meringues in oven to cool. Peel meringues off paper once they are cool.

To make mocha fondue, break up chocolate into a fondue pot, add coffee and cream, and heat gently until melted, stirring all the time. Stir in Tia Maria and beat until smooth. Leave pot over a lighted spirit burner to keep warm. Serve with nutty meringues and fruit.

Serves 6.

CHOCOLATE NUT FONDUE

12oz Swiss chocolate with nuts
1 cup heavy cream
2 tablespoons brandy or rum
selection of fresh fruit, to serve
VIENNESE FINGERS:
½ cup butter
2 tablespoons confectioners' sugar
1 cup all-purpose flour
¼ teaspoon baking powder
few drops vanilla extract

To make Viennese fingers, preheat oven to 375F (190C). Grease 2 or 3 baking sheets. Beat butter and confectioners' sugar together in a bowl until pale and creamy.

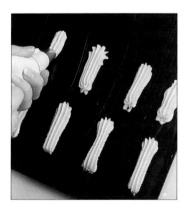

Add sifted flour, baking powder, and vanilla extract and beat well. Put mixture into a pastry bag fitted with ¼ inch star tube and pipe 2 inch fingers on to greased baking sheets, to make a total of 24. Bake in the oven for 15 minutes. Leave to cool on a wire rack.

To make chocolate fondue, break up chocolate into a fondue pot. Add cream and heat gently, stirring all the time until chocolate melts. Stir in brandy or rum, then leave over a lighted spirit burner to keep warm. Serve with Viennese fingers and fruit.

Serves 6.

BANANA & CHOCOLATE BITES

6 firm ripe bananas
¼ cup shelled pistachio nuts
8oz dark chocolate
4 tablespoons light cream

Peel bananas and cut them into 1 inch lengths. Cover a metal baking sheet with plastic wrap.

Arrange banana slices in a single layer on the baking sheet and place in the freezer. Leave in the freezer for at least 3 hours or until completely frozen. Coarsely chop pistachio nuts and divide between 4 small shallow dishes. When ready to serve, break up chocolate into the fondue pot. Add cream and heat gently on top of the stove, stirring, until chocolate is melted and mixture is smooth.

Transfer fondue pot to the lighted spirit burner. Bring banana pieces to the table on the metal baking sheet. To serve, spear the banana on to bamboo skewers or fondue forks, dip into the chocolate, and then into the chopped nuts.

Serves 6.

CHOCOLATE ORANGE FONDUE

12oz dark chocolate chips
4 tablespoons heavy cream
¼ cup orange juice
1 teaspoon grated orange rind
PROFITEROLES:
¼ cup butter
2½oz all-purpose flour, sifted
2 eggs, lightly beaten
⅔ cup heavy cream, whipped

Preheat the oven to 425F (220C). Butter 2 baking sheets. Make the profiteroles. Place butter in a pan with ⅔ cup water. Bring just to a boil and remove from the heat.

Add flour to pan, stirring constantly with a wooden spoon, until combined. (See above.) Return pan to heat and continue beating over a low heat until mixture is smooth and pulls away from sides of the pan. Remove from heat and leave to cool for a minute. Beat in eggs, a little at a time, until mixture is smooth and glossy. Using 2 spoons, place 24 walnut-size mounds of mixture well apart on the baking sheets. Bake for 20 minutes until well risen and golden brown. Reduce oven temperature to 350F (180C). Make a hole in each bun.

Return buns to the oven for 5 minutes. Cool on a wire rack. Spoon a little cream into each bun. Place chocolate chips, cream, and orange juice in a large microwave-safe bowl. Cover and microwave at full power for 1 minute. Stir until smooth. Heat for a few more seconds, if necessary, until all the chocolate is melted. Stir in orange rind. Transfer to a fondue pot and place on a lighted burner. Spear profiteroles on to bamboo skewers or fondue forks, to serve.

Serves 4-6.

BLACK FOREST FONDUE

14oz can pitted black cherries
⅔ cup heavy cream
1 tablespoon kirsch
1 tablespoon cornstarch
CHOCOLATE CAKE:
2 eggs
½ cup softened butter
½ cup superfine sugar
1 cup self rising flour
½ teaspoon baking powder
2 tablespoons cocoa
1 tablespoon milk

Preheat the oven to 375F (190C). Grease an 8-inch shallow, square pan.

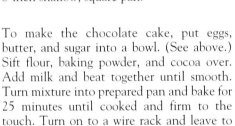

To make the chocolate cake, put eggs, butter, and sugar into a bowl. (See above.) Sift flour, baking powder, and cocoa over. Add milk and beat together until smooth. Turn mixture into prepared pan and bake for 25 minutes until cooked and firm to the touch. Turn on to a wire rack and leave to cool. Cut into small squares when cold.

Empty cherries and their juice into a blender or food processor, and process until reasonably smooth. Transfer to a fondue pot, stir in cream, and heat until simmering. Add kirsch. In a small bowl, blend together cornstarch and 1 tablespoon of water. Add to the fondue pot and continue to cook, stirring, until the mixture thickens. Transfer the fondue pot to the lighted spirit burner. Serve with the chocolate cake to dip in.

Serves 4.

PRALINE FONDUE

½ cup superfine sugar
¾ cup blanched almonds
8oz white chocolate
⅔ cup heavy cream
few drops vanilla extract
cubes of cake and a selection of fresh fruit, to serve

To make praline, oil a baking sheet. Put sugar and almonds into a small heavy saucepan. Place over a low heat and leave until sugar becomes liquid and golden. Pour at once on to oiled baking sheet, then leave to cool and harden for 15 minutes.

Coarsely break up praline, then put into a blender or food processor and process until finely ground.

Put chocolate and cream into a fondue pot and heat gently until chocolate melts, stirring all the time. Stir in praline, and flavor with a few drops of extract. Serve with cubes of cake and pieces of fresh fruit.

Serves 6.

TIRAMISU FONDUE

generous 1 cup mascarpone cheese
2 tablespoons rum
3½oz dark chocolate
1 tablespoon instant coffee granules
1 tablespoon superfine sugar (optional)
TO SERVE:
squares of panettone
Italian ladyfingers
strawberries

Place mascarpone cheese in the fondue pot with the rum. Heat gently on top of the stove, stirring, until mascarpone melts.

Break up chocolate into small pieces and add to the fondue pot. Continue to heat gently until chocolate melts.

Add coffee granules and stir until mixture is smooth. Taste the fondue and add sugar if desired. Transfer the fondue pot to the lighted spirit burner and serve with panettone, ladyfingers, and strawberries.

Serves 4.

BANOFFEE FONDUE

9oz vanilla fudge
1¼ cups heavy cream
sliced bananas, to serve
MINI CHOCOLATE MUFFINS:
1½oz dark chocolate
1¼ cups all-purpose flour
1½ teaspoons baking powder
pinch salt
½ teaspoon ground cinnamon
¼ cup superfine sugar
1 egg
½ cup milk
¼ cup butter, melted and cooled slightly

Preheat the oven to 400F (200C).

Arrange 20 petit-four cases on a baking sheet. To make the muffins, chop the chocolate into small pieces. Sift the flour, baking powder, salt and cinnamon into a bowl. In another bowl, whisk together the sugar, egg, milk and melted butter. Add the dry ingredients and the chocolate and fold together quickly and lightly until just combined. Divide the mixture between the petit-four cases and bake in the oven for 15minutes or until well risen and golden. Transfer to a wire rack to cool.

To make the fondue, place the fudge and cream in the fondue pot and heat gently, stirring until melted and smooth. Transfer the fondue pot to the lighted burner. To serve, spear the banana and muffin cakes on to bamboo skewers or fondue forks.

Serves 6.

CAPPUCCINO FONDUE

8oz white chocolate
¼ cup strong espresso coffee
⅔ cup heavy cream
drinking chocolate, for sprinkling
PISTACHIO BISCOTTI:
2 cups all-purpose flour
1 teaspoon baking powder
pinch salt
¾ cup superfine sugar
2 eggs
grated rind 1 lemon
1 tablespoon lemon juice
¾ cup blanched almonds, toasted and roughly
   chopped
⅓ cup shelled pistachio nuts, roughly chopped

Preheat the oven to 350F (180C). Line a baking sheet with non-stick parchment. To make biscotti, sift flour, baking powder, and salt into a mixing bowl. Stir in sugar, eggs, lemon rind and juice, and nuts. Mix together to form a firm dough. (See above.) Roll dough into a ball, cut in half, and roll each portion into a roll about 1¼ inches in diameter. Place rolls on the baking sheet at least 3½ inches apart. Lightly flatten rolls and bake for 15-20 minutes until golden brown. Remove from oven and leave to cool and firm up for 5 minutes.

With a serrated knife, cut biscotti at an angle into ½ inch thick slices. Arrange slices on baking sheet and return to the oven for a further 15 minutes, turning once. Transfer to a wire rack to cool. To make the fondue, place chocolate, coffee, and cream in the fondue pot and heat gently on top of the stove until chocolate has melted and mixture is smooth. Sprinkle with drinking chocolate then transfer to the lighted spirit burner and serve with the biscotti.

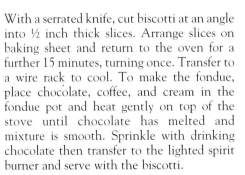

Serves 4.

TOFFEE FONDUE

¼ cup butter
¾ cup soft brown sugar
4 tablespoons golden syrup or corn syrup
14oz can evaporated milk
4 tablespoons chopped unsalted peanuts
6 teaspoons cornstarch
pieces of apple, pear, and banana, and popcorn, to
  serve

Put butter, sugar, and syrup into a saucepan and heat gently until mixture begins to bubble, stirring occasionally. Allow to boil for 1 minute.

Stir in evaporated milk and cook for 3-4 minutes until sauce is hot and boiling, then add chopped nuts.

In a small bowl, blend cornstarch smoothly with 2 tablespoons water. Add mixture to sauce in pan and heat until thickened, stirring. Pour into a fondue pot and place over a burner to keep warm. Serve with pieces of apple, pear, and banana, and popcorn.

Serves 4-6.

BUTTERSCOTCH FONDUE

¼ cup unsalted butter
¾ cup soft brown sugar
2 tablespoons golden syrup or corn syrup
½ teaspoon grated lemon rind
1 teaspoon lemon juice
2 tablespoons cornstarch
14oz can evaporated milk
fresh fruit, to serve
VANILLA COOKIES:
1 vanilla bean
½ cup unsalted butter
⅓ cup superfine sugar
1 egg yolk
1 cup self rising flour

To make the cookies, slit vanilla bean lengthwise and scrape black seeds into a large bowl. (See above.) Add butter and sugar, and beat together until light and fluffy. Beat in egg yolk, then stir in flour to make a stiff dough. Wrap dough in plastic wrap and chill for 15 minutes. Preheat the oven to 375F (190C). Grease 2 or 3 baking sheets. Divide dough into 30 small balls and place well apart on baking sheets. Flatten slightly. Bake for 15 minutes until golden brown. Transfer to wire racks to cool.

To make fondue, place butter, sugar, syrup, and lemon rind and juice in a fondue pot and heat gently until sugar has dissolved. Boil for 1 minute. Blend cornstarch and 2 tablespoons of the evaporated milk. Stir remaining evaporated milk into sugar mixture. Heat until just simmering then simmer for 2-3 minutes. Stir in blended cornstarch then bring to a boil, stirring, until smooth and thick. Transfer to the lighted burner and serve with cookies and fruit.

Serves 6.

FRUITS OF THE FOREST FONDUE

1lb 2oz package of frozen fruits of the forest or
  summer fruits
4 tablespoons confectioners' sugar
2 tablespoons crème de cassis or kirsch
2 tablespoons cornstarch
scant 1 cup fromage frais
MINI LEMON CAKES:
2 eggs
½ cup softened butter
½ cup superfine sugar
1 cup self rising flour
grated rind 1 lemon
1 tablespoon lemon juice

Preheat the oven to 375F (190C). Arrange
40 paper petit-four cases on a baking sheet.
(See above.) To make lemon cakes, put eggs,
butter, and sugar into a bowl. Sift flour over.
Add lemon rind and juice, and beat together
until smooth. Put a teaspoon of mixture in
each of the petit-four cases and bake for
10-15 minutes until cooked and firm to the
touch. Leave to cool on a wire rack before
removing from the paper cases.

Process fruit and any juice in a blender or food
processor, then press through a sieve into a
fondue pot. Stir in confectioners' sugar; heat
gently on the stove until almost simmering.
Blend together crème de cassis or kirsch and
cornstarch and stir into fruit purée. Cook,
stirring, for 2-3 minutes until thickened. Stir
in fromage frais and heat gently, stirring, until
well blended. Transfer the fondue pot to the
lighted spirit burner and serve with lemon
cakes for dipping.

Serves 6.

HOT BERRY COMPOTE

1lb 2oz mixed summer fruits such as red currants,
  black currants, and raspberries
½ cup superfine sugar
pinch mixed spice
6 teaspoons cornstarch
LANGUE-DE-CHAT COOKIES:
½ cup butter
½ cup superfine sugar
2 eggs
1½ cups self rising flour

To make cookies, preheat oven to 425F
(220C). Grease 2 or 3 baking sheets. Beat
butter and sugar together until pale and
fluffy; beat in eggs and work in flour.

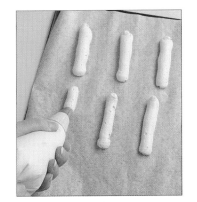

Put mixture into a pastry bag fitted with a
½ inch plain tube and pipe 2½ inch fingers
on to greased baking sheets (spaced well
apart) to make a batch of 24-30. Bake in the
oven for about 8 minutes until light golden.
Cool on a wire rack.

To make fondue, put fruits into a saucepan
with sugar and ⅔ cup water and cook gently
until tender. Crush fruits slightly with a
potato masher and add mixed spice. In a
small bowl, blend cornstarch smoothly with
a little water. Add to fruit in pan and cook
until thickened, stirring all the time. Pour
into a fondue pot and place over a lighted
spirit burner. Serve with langue-de-chat
cookies.

Serves 6.

LEMON MERINGUE FONDUE

4 tablespoons cornstarch
1¼ cups coconut milk
grated rind and juice 2 lemons
¼ cup superfine sugar
pieces of mango, to serve
MERINGUES:
2 egg whites
½ cup superfine sugar
½ teaspoon vanilla extract

Preheat the oven to 225F (110C). Line 2 or 3 baking sheets with non-stick paper. Put egg whites in a large clean bowl and whisk until meringue holds soft peaks.

Add sugar, 1 tablespoonful at a time, whisking well after each addition. Continue whisking until stiff and glossy. Fold in vanilla with a rubber spatula. Put 24 teaspoonfuls of mixture on to lined baking sheets. Bake for 1-1½ hours until dry and crisp. Turn off oven and leave meringues in oven to cool. Remove from the paper when cool.

To make the fondue, put cornstarch and a little of the coconut milk in the fondue pot and stir to make a paste. Stir in remaining coconut milk. Bring to a boil on top of the stove, stirring, and continue to cook for 2-3 minutes until thickened. Remove from heat, and add lemon rind and juice, and sugar. Reheat then transfer the fondue pot to the lighted spirit burner. Serve with the mango and meringues.

Serves 4-6.

RASPBERRY CREAM

1lb raspberries, thawed if frozen
4 teaspoons cornstarch
1¼ cups light cream
⅓ cup confectioners' sugar
3 tablespoons Framboise (optional)
QUICK MERINGUES:
2 egg whites
⅔ cup confectioners' sugar

Rub raspberries through a sieve and discard seeds. Keep purée on one side.

To make the meringues, preheat oven to 325F (160C). Line a baking sheet with non-stick paper. Place egg whites and confectioners' sugar in a bowl over a pan of hot water and, with an electric whisk, whisk until mixture is stiff and standing in peaks. Place mixture in a pastry bag fitted with a ½ inch star tube and pile small blobs on to lined baking sheet. Bake in the oven for 10-15 minutes until crisp on the outside. Allow to cool before removing from paper.

In a saucepan, blend the cornstarch smoothly with a little of the cream. Stir in the remainder and add sugar and raspberry purée. Cook over a gentle heat until smooth and thickened. Stir in the Framboise, if desired, then pour into a fondue pot and serve with small meringues. Serve hot or cold.

Serves 4-6.

SWEET CHERRY COMPOTE

2 x 15oz cans red cherries
6 teaspoons cornstarch
⅓ cup superfine sugar
3 tablespoons cherry brandy
ice cream, to serve
FANCY CAKES:
¼ cup butter
2 eggs, separated
¼ cup superfine sugar
½ cup all-purpose flour
grated rind ½ lemon

To make cakes, preheat oven to 375F (190C). Grease and flour a 12 hole muffin pan. Warm butter in a pan until just melting.

Whisk egg yolks and sugar until pale and creamy. Lightly fold in sifted flour, lemon rind, and butter until thoroughly mixed. Whisk egg whites until stiff and fold into mixture. Spoon mixture into greased and floured muffin pan. Bake in the oven for 10 minutes or until golden and firm to touch. Turn out and cool on a wire rack.

To make the compote, drain cherries, reserving juice, and remove pits. In a saucepan, blend cornstarch smoothly with a little of the reserved juice, then add the remainder and stir in sugar. Cook over a medium heat until the sauce has thickened, stirring all the time. Stir in cherries and brandy. Reheat, then pour into the fondue pot over a lighted spirit burner. Serve with a small ladle to pour over ice cream and fancy cakes.

Serves 6.

FRUIT SURPRISES

12oz frozen puff pastry, thawed
8oz can pineapple slices, drained and juice reserved
⅓ cup glacé cherries, chopped
1oz angelica, chopped
oil, for cooking
RUM SAUCE:
4 oranges
3 teaspoons cornstarch
⅓ cup soft brown sugar
6 teaspoons butter, diced
4 tablespoons dark rum

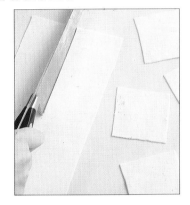

On a lightly floured surface, roll out pastry thinly; cut into eighteen 3 inch squares.

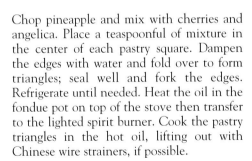

Chop pineapple and mix with cherries and angelica. Place a teaspoonful of mixture in the center of each pastry square. Dampen the edges with water and fold over to form triangles; seal well and fork the edges. Refrigerate until needed. Heat the oil in the fondue pot on top of the stove then transfer to the lighted spirit burner. Cook the pastry triangles in the hot oil, lifting out with Chinese wire strainers, if possible.

To make rum sauce, finely grate rind from one of the oranges, then squeeze juice from all of them. Put cornstarch in a saucepan, add reserved pineapple juice and blend together smoothly. Add sugar and orange juice and stir well. Bring to a boil, stirring all the time and simmer for 2 minutes. Whisk in butter, orange rind, and rum. Serve hot with the hot pastry triangles.

Serves 6.

STRAWBERRY ROULÉ DIP

SPICED APRICOT FONDUE

14oz can strawberries, drained
8oz strawberry roulé cheese
⅔ cup heavy cream
fresh strawberries and Quick Almond Sponge (see page 81), to serve

2 x 14oz cans apricot halves in natural juice
1 sachet wine mulling spices or 1 tablespoon mulling spices tied in muslin
2 tablespoons cornstarch
1¼ cups fromage frais
kiwi fruit, to serve
ALMOND MACAROONS:
2 extra large egg whites
¼ cup ground almonds
½ cup superfine sugar
1 tablespoon cornstarch
few drops almond extract
24 split blanched almonds

Put strawberries and cheese into a blender or food processor and blend until smooth.

Preheat the oven to 375F (190C).

In a bowl, whip the cream until softly peaking, the fold in the strawberry cheese mixture. Turn mixture into a serving bowl.

Line 2 or 3 baking sheets with non-stick paper. Make the macaroons. Reserve 2 teaspoons of egg white for brushing. In a large bowl, whisk remaining egg whites until frothy. (See above.) Stir in almonds, sugar, cornstarch, and almond extract. Mix together well. Place 24 small spoonfuls of mixture on to baking sheets. Smooth out slightly with the back of a spoon. Place a split blanched almond in center of each macaroon and brush the top with reserved egg white. Bake for 10-15 minutes until a pale golden brown. Leave for 5 minutes then cool on a wire rack.

Hull strawberries, if desired, and arrange on a serving plate with cubes of almond sponge. Spear a strawberry or a piece of sponge on fondue forks and dunk in the dip.

Serves 4-6.

Place apricots and juice in fondue pot with spice sachet. Heat until simmering then remove from heat and leave to cool. Remove sachet, and place apricots and juice in a blender or food processor. Process to a purée and return to fondue pot. Reheat gently. In a small bowl, blend cornstarch with a little water. Add to apricot purée and continue to heat, stirring, until thickened. Stir in fromage frais then transfer fondue pot to lighted burner. Serve with kiwi fruit and macaroons.

Serves 4-6.

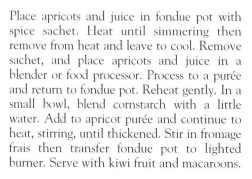

SPICED PLUM PURÉE

1½lb red or yellow plums
½ cup sugar
½ teaspoon ground cinnamon
4 teaspoons cornstarch
2 tablespoons ginger wine
Lemon Sponge (see page 86), and slices of apple and
   pear, to serve

Cut plums in half; discard pits. Put plums into a saucepan with sugar and cinnamon and 1¼ cups water. Cover and simmer for 15 minutes.

Press the fruit mixture through a sieve into a fondue pot.

In a small bowl, blend cornstarch smoothly with wine and stir into plum purée. Heat gently, stirring until thickened. Serve with small squares of lemon sponge and slices of apple and pear to dip into the purée.

Serves 4-6.

APRICOT YOGURT DIP

8oz ready-to-eat dried apricots
2 tablespoons Amaretto liqueur
⅔ cup plain yogurt
QUICK ALMOND SPONGE:
2 eggs
½ cup soft margarine
½ cup superfine sugar
1 cup self rising flour
pinch baking powder
few drops almond extract

Put apricots into a bowl, cover with 1¼ cups water and leave to soak for 2-3 hours.

To make quick almond sponge, preheat oven to 350F (180C). Grease an 8-inch shallow, square cake pan. Put all the ingredients for sponge into a bowl and beat with a wooden spoon for 3 minutes. Turn mixture into greased pan and bake in the oven for 25 minutes or until golden brown and firm to the touch. Turn on to a wire rack and leave to cool. Cut into small squares when cold.

Drain apricots (reserving liquor) and put into a blender or food processor with the Amaretto and yogurt. Blend until smooth. If mixture is a little too thick, add a small amount of reserved apricot liquor. Spoon into a fondue pot and heat over a lighted spirit burner to serve warm with the pieces of cake.

Serves 4-6.

Note: The dip can also be served cold.

STRAWBERRY & CREAM FONDUE

½ cup strawberries
confectioners' sugar
13oz white chocolate
1 cup heavy cream
2 tablespoons framboise or kirsch
fresh strawberries, to serve

Place strawberries in a blender or food processor and process until smooth. Press through a sieve into a bowl. Add confectioners' sugar to taste.

Roughly chop or break up chocolate into pieces and place in the fondue pot. Add the heavy cream. Over a low heat, heat gently, stirring continuously, until chocolate melts. Add the framboise or kirsch, and stir until smooth.

Place the fondue pot over a lighted spirit burner to keep warm. Swirl the strawberry purée on the surface of the cream sauce. Serve with fresh strawberries.

Serves 6.

BLACK CURRANT FONDUE

1½lb black currants, topped and tailed if fresh;
  thawed if frozen
½ cup superfine sugar
3 teaspoons cornstarch
2 tablespoons light cream
4 tablespoons Cassis
HAZELNUT MACAROONS:
2 egg whites
½ cup light soft brown sugar
1⅔ cups ground hazelnuts
¼ cup finely chopped hazelnuts

To make macaroons, preheat oven to 350F (180C). Line 3 baking sheets with non-stick paper. Whisk egg whites until softly peaking. Fold in sugar and ground nuts.

Place spoonfuls on to lined baking sheets to make a total of 24. Sprinkle with chopped nuts and bake in the oven for 15-20 minutes until crisp and firm to the touch.

To make the fondue, put black currants into a saucepan with sugar and ⅔ cup water and cook gently until tender. Press mixture through a sieve into a fondue pot. In a small bowl, blend cornstarch smoothly with cream and stir into the purée together with Cassis. Reheat until thickened, stirring frequently. Serve with hazelnut macaroons.

Serves 4-6.

FRUIT FRITTERS

2 bananas, cut into 1 inch pieces
2 eating apples, cored and cut into chunks
2 teaspoons lemon juice
1 small, fresh pineapple, peeled and cut into chunks
oil, for cooking
½ cup superfine sugar mixed with
  1 teaspoon ground cinnamon, to serve
BATTER:
1 cup all-purpose flour
pinch salt
1 egg
⅔ cup milk

Toss bananas and apples in lemon juice, then arrange on a plate with pineapple.

To make batter, sift flour and salt into a bowl. Beat in egg, then gradually add milk, beating to make a smooth batter. Heat oil in the fondue pot on top of the stove then transfer to the lighted spirit burner.

The fritters are cooked at the table by spearing the fruit with a fondue fork, dipping it in the batter, and cooking in the hot oil. Pat each fritter on paper towels, then dip in cinnamon sugar mixture before eating.

Serves 6.

Note: To add extra color, decorate cinnamon sugar with a sprig of mint or pineapple leaves, if desired.

PEPPERMINT FONDUE

2½ cups light cream
1 cup confectioners' sugar
6 teaspoons cornstarch
peppermint extract, to taste
MINI CHOCOLATE CAKES:
2 eggs
½ cup soft margarine
½ cup superfine sugar
1 cup self rising flour
6 teaspoons cocoa
3 teaspoons milk

To make chocolate cakes, preheat oven to 375F (190C). Put all ingredients into a bowl and beat together until smooth.

Put teaspoonfuls of mixture into 40 petits fours cases on a baking sheet. Bake in the oven for 15 minutes until cooked. Leave to cool on a wire rack before removing from paper cases.

Put cream and sugar into a saucepan and heat gently until almost boiling. Blend cornstarch smoothly with 1 tablespoon water, add to cream, and continue to heat, stirring all the time, until thickened. Add extract, to taste, then pour into a fondue pot and serve hot with mini chocolate cakes.

Serves 6.

COCONUT DIP

1 cup desiccated coconut
2oz creamed coconut, chopped
¼ cup sugar
4 teaspoons cornstarch
⅔ cup light cream
MINI FLAPJACKS:
½ cup margarine
4 tablespoons honey
½ cup soft brown sugar
2 cups porridge oats
⅓ cup chopped blanched almonds

To make flapjacks, preheat oven to 350F (180C). In a saucepan, melt margarine, honey, and sugar. Add oats and nuts; mix well.

Using a teaspoon, spoon mixture into 48 petits fours cases on a baking sheet. Bake in the oven for 20 minutes until golden. Leave to cool.

To make dip, put desiccated coconut in a saucepan with 2¼ cups water, the creamed coconut, and sugar. Bring to a boil and simmer for 10 minutes. Strain mixture into a bowl, pressing mixture thoroughly to extract all liquid. In a fondue pot, blend cornstarch smoothly with cream, then add coconut liquid and cook over a gentle heat until thickened, stirring all the time. Serve warm with mini flapjacks.

Serves 6.

SABAYON SAUCE

4 large, ripe, firm eating pears
½ cup Marsala
3 egg yolks
⅓ cup superfine sugar
3 teaspoons brandy

Preheat oven to 350F (180C). Peel, halve, and core pears, and slice thickly. Put in an ovenproof dish, pour Marsala over, then cover and bake in the oven for 20 minutes.

Drain off juice from pears and reserve. Place egg yolks and sugar in a bowl and whisk until pale and frothy. Add reserved juice from pears, then place bowl over a pan of simmering water and whisk until mixture is thick.

Remove bowl from pan, stir in brandy, and serve immediately, with the pear slices for dipping.

Serves 4-6.

GOOSEBERRY WINE FONDUE

RHUBARB & CUSTARD FONDUE

1½lb gooseberries, trimmed
1½ cup superfine sugar
⅔ cup dry white wine
2 teaspoons cornstarch
2 tablespoons light cream
BRANDY SNAPS:
¼ cup butter
⅓ cup soft brown sugar
2 tablespoons golden syrup or corn syrup
½ cup all-purpose flour
½ teaspoon ground ginger

To make brandy snaps, preheat oven to 350F (180C). Melt butter, sugar, and syrup in a saucepan.

Cool slightly, then beat in flour and ginger. Place 4 teaspoonfuls of mixture on to a baking sheet, spaced well apart, and bake in the oven for 10 minutes. Repeat with remaining mixture, to make a total of 24. Leave each batch to cool slightly on baking sheet before removing with a palette knife and rolling around clean, greased pencils or chopsticks. Allow to cool and set before removing.

Put gooseberries into a saucepan with sugar and wine. Simmer until tender. Reserve a few gooseberries for decoration, then pass remainder through a sieve to make a purée. In a fondue pot, blend cornstarch smoothly with cream. Stir in gooseberry purée, then heat until smooth and thick, stirring frequently. Decorate with reserved gooseberries and serve with brandy snaps.

Serves 4-6.

1¼lb cans rhubarb in syrup
2 cups fresh custard
GINGER SPONGE:
2 eggs
½ cup softened butter
½ cup golden superfine sugar
1 cup self rising flour
1 teaspoon ground ginger
pinch baking powder
2 pieces ginger from a jar of stem ginger in syrup, finely chopped
1 tablespoon syrup from the ginger jar

Preheat oven to 350F (180C). Grease an 8-inch shallow, square cake pan.

To make the ginger sponge, put eggs, butter, and superfine sugar in a bowl. Sift flour, ginger, and baking powder into the bowl. Add chopped ginger and syrup, and beat together until thoroughly blended. (See above.) Turn the mixture into the prepared pan and bake for 25 minutes or until golden and firm to the touch. Leave in the pan for 5 minutes then turn out on to a wire rack to cool. Cut into small squares when cold.

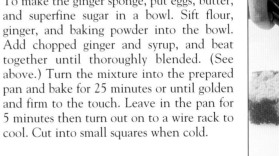

To make the fondue, drain rhubarb and place in a blender or food processor. Process to a purée then place in the fondue pot with the custard. Heat on top of the stove until hot but not boiling. Transfer the fondue pot to the lighted spirit burner and serve with the ginger sponge.

Serves 4-6.

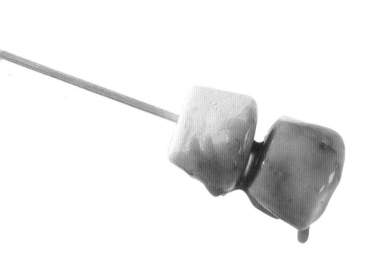

MARSHMALLOW FONDUE

8oz marshmallows
⅔ cup bottled raspberry or strawberry sauce
⅔ cup heavy cream
1-2 tablespoons lemon juice (optional)
TO SERVE:
marshmallows
ladyfingers
strawberries

Using wet scissors, snip marshmallows into pieces and place in the fondue pot.

Add fruit sauce and cream. Place over a very low heat and cook gently, stirring, until marshmallows have melted and mixture is smooth.

Add lemon juice, to taste, if desired. Transfer the fondue pot to the lighted spirit burner and serve with marshmallows, ladyfingers, and strawberries.

Serves 4.

DRAMBUIE CREAM FONDUE

4 teaspoons cornstarch
1¼ cups heavy cream
3 teaspoons superfine sugar
3 tablespoons Drambuie
3 oranges, peeled and segmented, to serve
LEMON SPONGE:
2 eggs
½ cup soft margarine
½ cup superfine sugar
1 cup self rising flour
pinch baking powder
finely grated rind and juice ½ lemon

Preheat oven to 350F (180C). Put all ingredients for sponge in a bowl.

Beat together for 3 minutes. Grease an 8-inch shallow, square cake pan. Turn mixture into greased cake pan. Bake in the oven for 25 minutes or until golden and firm to the touch. Turn on to a wire rack and leave to cool. Cut into small squares when cold.

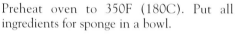

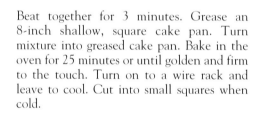

To make fondue, in a saucepan, blend cornstarch smoothly with cream. Cook over gentle heat until thickened and smooth, stirring all the time. Stir in sugar and Drambuie, then pour into a serving dish. Serve with segments of orange and squares of lemon sponge.

Serves 6.

Note: Cut the rind from oranges into strips to decorate, if desired.

SAUCES
& SALADS

ROUILLE

2 slices white bread, crusts removed
2 red bell peppers, seeded and quartered
2 fresh red chilies, seeded and chopped
2 cloves garlic, crushed
olive oil

Place bread in a shallow dish with 3-4 tablespoons cold water and soak for 10 minutes.

Broil red bell pepper quarters, skin side up, until the skin is charred and blistered. Place in a plastic bag until cool enough to handle. Peel off skins and chop flesh roughly.

Place red bell pepper flesh in a blender or food processor. Drain the bread and squeeze out the excess moisture. Add to bell peppers with chilies and garlic. Process to a coarse paste then gradually add enough olive oil to give the desired consistency. Transfer to small serving bowls.

Serves 4-6.

CHILI TOMATO SAUCE

1 onion
2 stalks celery
1 clove garlic
1 red bell pepper
1 red chili
2 tablespoons oil
14oz canned chopped tomatoes
1 teaspoon molasses or dark soft brown sugar
salt and freshly ground black pepper
chopped fresh cilantro, to garnish

Finely chop the onion and celery stalks. Crush garlic and seed red bell pepper and chop. Core and seed the chili and chop very finely.

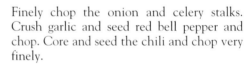

Heat oil in a saucepan. Add onion, celery, garlic, and red bell pepper, and cook for 10 minutes until soft. Add chili, tomatoes, and molasses, and season with salt and pepper.

Bring to a boil, cover, and simmer gently for 20-30 minutes until thickened and well blended. Garnish with chopped cilantro.

Serves 4-6.

TWO MAYONNAISES

SAFFRON MAYONNAISE:
⅔ cup fish stock
½ teaspoon saffron strands
⅔ cup mayonnaise
1 teaspoon lemon juice
salt and freshly ground black pepper

AIOLI:
⅔ cup mayonnaise
2 cloves garlic, crushed
1 teaspoon Dijon mustard
salt and freshly ground black pepper (optional)

To make the saffron mayonnaise, put fish stock in a saucepan and bring to a boil.

Boil until reduced to 1 tablespoon. Add saffron strands and leave to cool. Strain stock into a bowl and stir in mayonnaise. Add lemon juice and season with salt and pepper. (Salt will not be needed if the fish stock was salty.) Spoon into a serving bowl, cover and chill until required.

To make the aioli, place mayonnaise, garlic, and mustard in a bowl. Mix together and season with salt and pepper, if desired. Transfer to a serving bowl, cover and chill until required. Set aside.

Serves 4.

CUMBERLAND SAUCE

1 shallot
1 orange
1 lemon
⅓ cup red currant jelly
1 teaspoon Dijon mustard
⅓ cup port
1 teaspoon arrowroot

Chop shallot very finely and place in a saucepan. With a peeler, remove the rind of orange and lemon.

Cut into very fine strips and add to the pan. Cover with cold water, bring to a boil, and cook for 5 minutes. Drain and set aside. Meanwhile, halve orange and lemon and squeeze juice. Set aside. Add red currant jelly to the pan and heat gently, stirring until melted.

Stir in mustard, port, juice of orange and lemon, blanched rind, and shallot. Cook for about 5 minutes. In a small bowl, mix arrowroot to a paste with a 1 tablespoon of cold water. Add to the sauce in the pan. Simmer for a further 2-3 minutes until slightly thickened then leave to cool before serving.

Serves 4.

TOMATO & OLIVE SALSA

4 plum tomatoes
1¼ cups mixed pitted green and black olives, roughly
   chopped
1 small red onion, finely chopped
1 fresh red chili, seeded and finely chopped
2 tablespoons olive oil
salt and freshly ground black pepper

To peel the tomatoes, cut a cross in the rounded side of each tomato.

Place them in a bowl and pour boiling water over to cover. Leave for 1 minute then drain and cover with cold water. Leave for 1 more minute, then remove and peel. Cut tomatoes into quarters and remove cores, then cut tomato flesh into tiny dice and place in a bowl.

Add olives, onion, and chili to tomatoes in the bowl. Stir in olive oil and season with salt and pepper. Transfer to a serving bowl and serve.

Serves 4.

AVOCADO & MELON SALSA

1 ripe avocado
½ canteloupe melon
juice 1 lime
4 scallions, very finely chopped
1 fresh red chili, seeded, and very finely chopped
salt and freshly ground black pepper
mint leaves, to garnish

Cut the avocado in half. Remove the stone and peel off the skin.

Remove seeds from melon and cut away skin. Cut avocado and melon into small dice and place in a bowl with lime juice. Toss together well. Add scallions and chili. Season with salt and pepper.

Cover closely with plastic wrap and leave to stand for 30 minutes. (Do not leave for longer than this or the avocado will discolor.) Transfer to a serving dish. Roughly tear or chop the mint leaves and scatter over the salsa before serving.

Serves 4.

VARIATION: Any type of melon can be used as long as it is ripe and has a good flavor. You should have 8oz melon after peeling and seeding.

CHOW MEIN SALAD

4oz Chinese medium egg noodles
4oz snow peas
6oz fresh bean sprouts
½ bunch scallions, chopped
1 red bell pepper, seeded and sliced
4oz button mushrooms, sliced
1 small Little Gem lettuce, shredded
SESAME DRESSING:
4 tablespoons sunflower oil
2 tablespoons lemon juice
3 teaspoons soy sauce
1 inch piece of fresh ginger root
2 tablespoons sesame seeds

Break up noodles and cook in boiling, salted water for 5-6 minutes.

Drain noodles and leave to cool. Top and tail snow peas, then break in half and put into a bowl. Pour over enough boiling water to cover and leave to stand for 2 minutes; drain and cool. Put noodles and snow peas into a salad bowl and add remaining salad ingredients.

In a bowl, combine oil, lemon juice, and soy sauce. Peel and cut ginger into very thin slivers and add to bowl. Mix ingredients together thoroughly and pour over salad. Toss together. Sprinkle with sesame seeds just before serving.

Serves 6-8.

COUSCOUS SALAD

3 tablespoons olive oil
5 scallions, chopped
1 clove garlic, crushed
1 teaspoon ground cumin
1½ cups vegetable stock
1 cup couscous
2 tomatoes, peeled and chopped
4 tablespoons chopped fresh parsley
4 tablespoons chopped fresh mint
1 fresh green chili, seeded and finely chopped
2 tablespoons lemon juice
salt and freshly ground black pepper
toasted pine nuts and grated lemon rind, to garnish

Heat oil in a saucepan. Add scallions and garlic.

Stir in cumin. Add stock and bring to a boil. Remove the pan from the heat and stir in couscous. Leave to stand for 10 minutes until couscous has absorbed all the liquid. Fluff up with a fork and transfer to a serving dish.

Leave to cool then stir in tomatoes, parsley, mint, chili, and lemon juice. Season with salt and pepper. Leave to stand for up to 1 hour to allow the flavors to develop. Scatter pine nuts and lemon rind over and serve.

Serves 4.

ORANGE & RED ONION SALAD

6 oranges
2 small red onions
1 tablespoon cumin seeds
1 teaspoon coarsely ground black pepper
1 tablespoon chopped fresh mint
6 tablespoons olive oil
salt
mint sprigs and black olives, to garnish

Working over a bowl to catch the juice, cut the skin away from oranges, removing the pith.

With a sharp knife, slice the oranges thinly. Slice onions across thinly, into rings, then separate the layers of the rings. Arrange the orange and onion slices in layers in a shallow dish. Sprinkle each layer with cumin seeds, black pepper, mint, olive oil, and salt to taste.

Pour any orange juice saved from slicing oranges over the salad. Leave in a cool place for about 2 hours, for the flavors to develop. Just before serving, scatter the salad with mint sprigs and black olives.

Serves 6.

VARIATION: Slices of fennel may be added to this salad.

SUMMER VEGETABLE SALAD

12oz eggplant, diced
salt and freshly ground black pepper
3 tablespoons olive oil
1 Spanish onion, sliced
12oz zucchini, sliced
1 red bell pepper, seeded and cut into chunks
1 green bell pepper, seeded and cut into chunks
1 yellow bell pepper, seeded and cut into chunks
3 tomatoes, peeled and chopped
1 tablespoon chopped fresh basil
1 tablespoon chopped fresh parsley (optional)

Put eggplant into a colander, sprinkle with salt, and leave to stand for 30 minutes. Rinse, drain, and pat dry.

Heat oil in a large skillet, add eggplant and onion, and cook over medium heat for 5 minutes. Add zucchini and bell peppers; cook over a low heat for 15 minutes, turning occasionally until tender.

Transfer vegetables to a bowl, stir in tomatoes, basil, and seasoning. Leave to cool, then chill. Serve sprinkled with chopped parsley, if desired.

Serves 6.

CARIBBEAN COLESLAW

ASIAN GREEN SALAD

1 red-leafed lettuce, such as oakleaf
½ iceberg lettuce, shredded
5 stalks celery, finely sliced
6oz carrots, grated
½ small pineapple, cut into chunks
3oz fresh dates, pitted and chopped
2oz walnuts or pecans, chopped
LIME DRESSING:
3 tablespoons mayonnaise
finely grated rind and juice 1 lime
6 teaspoons sunflower oil
salt and freshly ground black pepper

Line a large salad bowl or platter with red-leafed lettuce.

4oz snow peas, trimmed and halved
1 small head Chinese leaves
8 scallions, roughly chopped
1 green bell pepper, seeded and sliced
½ small cucumber
2 cups bean sprouts
2 tablespoons chopped roasted cashew nuts, and
  2 tablespoons chopped fresh cilantro, to garnish
GINGER & CHILI DRESSING:
1 inch piece fresh ginger root, grated
1 clove garlic, crushed
1 fresh red chili, seeded and finely chopped
1 teaspoon honey
grated rind and juice 1 lime
2 tablespoons oil
1 tablespoon soy sauce

In a bowl, put the remaining salad ingredients, except the nuts, and mix together. Mix dressing ingredients together, then pour over salad and toss lightly.

Bring a pan of water to a boil, add snow peas, cook for 2 minutes, then drain and refresh in cold water. (See above.) Drain again and place in a bowl. Finely shred Chinese leaves and add to the bowl with the scallions and green bell pepper.

Spoon salad into the prepared bowl or on to the platter and sprinkle with walnuts or pecans before serving.

Serves 6.

Peel cucumber, cut in half lengthwise and slice thinly. Add to the bowl with bean sprouts. To make the dressing, whisk together ginger, garlic, chili, honey, lime rind and juice, oil, and soy sauce. Pour over the salad and mix well. Transfer to a serving bowl. Before serving, scatter over chopped cashew nuts and cilantro.

Serves 4-6.

BEAN SALAD

14oz canned black-eyed peas
14oz canned red kidney beans
4 stalks celery, chopped
1 green bell pepper, seeded and roughly chopped
1 small red onion, finely chopped
4 tablespoons olive oil
1 tablespoon lime juice
1 teaspoon sugar
½-1 teaspoon hot pepper sauce
salt and freshly ground black pepper
2 tablespoons chopped fresh parsley

Drain and rinse black-eyed peas and red kidney beans. Place in a bowl.

Add the celery, green bell pepper, and onion to the black-eyed peas.

In a bowl, mix together olive oil, lime juice, sugar, and hot pepper sauce. Season with salt and pepper. Pour over the vegetable mixture and mix well. Set aside for 30 minutes then transfer to a serving dish. Scatter with chopped parsley and serve.

Serves 4-6.

VARIATIONS: The combination of beans can be varied according to preference and what is available.

RICE & SPINACH SALAD

2½ cups long-grain rice
2 tablespoons oil
1 bunch scallions, chopped
8oz frozen chopped spinach, thawed and well drained
salt and freshly ground black pepper
slice of lemon, to garnish

In a medium saucepan, bring 4 cups salted water to a boil. Keep water simmering while adding rice, then cover and cook for 15 minutes until rice is soft and water absorbed.

In a large saucepan, heat oil, add onions, and cook for 3-4 minutes, then stir into rice.

Add spinach and season with salt and pepper, then heat through for 1-2 minutes. Stir ingredients together and serve warm, garnished with a slice of lemon. Alternatively, serve the rice cold and fluff up with a fork before serving.

Serves 6.

INDEX

INDEX